Knowing Your Horse

Knowing Your Horse

A Guide to Equine Learning, Training and Behaviour

Emma Lethbridge, BSc (Hons), Dip PEB, BHSPT, EET, Cert CP

WILEY-BLACKWELL

A John Wiley & Sons, Ltd., Publication

This edition first published 2009
© 2009 Emma Lethbridge

Blackwell Publishing was acquired by John Wiley & Sons in February 2007. Blackwell's publishing programme has been merged with Wiley's global Scientific, Technical, and Medical business to form Wiley-Blackwell.

Registered office
John Wiley & Sons Ltd, The Atrium, Southern Gate, Chichester, West Sussex, PO19 8SQ, United Kingdom

Editorial offices
9600 Garsington Road, Oxford OX4 2DQ, United Kingdom
2121 State Avenue, Ames, Iowa 50014-8300, USA

For details of our global editorial offices, for customer services and for information about how to apply for permission to reuse the copyright material in this book please see our website at www.wiley.com/wiley-blackwell.

The right of the author to be identified as the author of this work has been asserted in accordance with the Copyright, Designs and Patents Act 1988.

Library of Congress Cataloging-in-Publication Data

Lethbridge, Emma.
  Knowing your horse : a guide to equine learning, training, and behaviour / Emma Lethbridge.
     p. cm.
  Includes bibliographical references and index.
  ISBN 978-1-4051-9164-7 (pbk. : alk. paper)   1. Horses–Behavior.
2. Horses–Training.   I. Title.
  SF281.L48 2009
  636.1'0835–dc22

                                                         2008044708

A catalogue record for this book is available from the British Library.

Set in 10.5/13pt Palatino by Graphicraft Limited, Hong Kong
Printed in Singapore by Ho Printing Singapore Pte Ltd

1   2009

Contents

Foreword

It has been said that empires have been won and lost on the back of the horse, and perhaps man owes a greater debt to the horse than any other species for assisting the spread of his culture between nations. Integral to this important relationship has been man's ability to ride the horse and, in so doing, get an animal to accept something extremely unnatural. The natural response of the horse to something on its back is resistance, because from an evolutionary point of view this has only ever signalled bad news in the form of a predator. While we have been riding horses for more than 5000 years it is important to remember this is not something that comes naturally to the horse, but is something that needs to be learned by every horse. It is testament to both the horse's trusting nature and its ability to learn that horse riding has been such a success. Indeed I never cease to be amazed at how well horses often seem to be able to pick out the correct intention of the confusing and often contradictory signals given by many a novice rider. However, we should not take this skill for granted, but rather we should accept our responsibility in this relationship. Part of this responsibility involves us not only understanding the nature of horses but also understanding the principles that allow us to help to shape this nature towards meeting our needs in as compassionate a way as possible.

There is no shortage of books trying to tell owners what to do, with a new name given to established techniques in order to generate a new product; sadly there are far fewer texts explaining the basic principles which are so often recycled into these methods, unfortunately sometimes with a confused understanding of the underlying science (Mills 1998). That is why this book is so important. As you read the text, you will soon become aware that Emma is a passionate horse lover, who genuinely takes the welfare of horses to heart, and she is also a scientist who understands both the theory and practice of learning and training. Perhaps what is less obvious is how rare it is to find this combination of characteristics in an individual who can write so clearly. She has brought together a wealth of knowledge with some of the latest research findings, to create an easy-to-read text. However, it is to be hoped that with this book, some of her skills will be less of a rarity and that many more will see and learn the value of understanding principles first and discover how much fun can be had simply training your horse. This can only be good for the horse and horse–human relationship. The importance of understanding the principles rather than applying techniques as if they were cooking recipes was brought home to me many years ago by an e-mail I received from a distraught owner who had just seen her horse break its neck and die after she did what she was told to do in order to control its pulling on the rope. No-one who cares about horses should put him or herself at risk of that situation and so this book is for owners who not only care about their horse, but also are willing to make a little effort to discover the true potential of their relationship. I can assure you your efforts will be more than rewarded.

This book blends good science effortlessly with practice, so that the reader can soon become a more skilled trainer. Simple scientific principles, like good record keeping, when applied to training, will teach you so much more as you apply what you read to your own horse and watch its response. If you understand the principles, then you are only limited by your imagination, and as you discover the many joys of training you will inevitably develop a deeper appreciation of horses. They do not lie and so you will also learn more about yourself. Horses are animals of immense beauty and grace and perhaps if we all took more time to appreciate these characteristics, we may find not only are we less stressed, but also our horses are less stressed. Don't rush, but rather savour the experience.

Daniel S. Mills BVSc PhD CBiol MIBiol ILTM CCAB Dip
ECVBM-CA MRCVS
Professor and RCVS Recognised and
European Specialist in Veterinary Behavioural Medicine
Department of Biological Sciences
University of Lincoln

REFERENCE

Mills, D.S. (1998) Applying learning theory to the management of the horse: the difference between getting it right and getting it wrong. *Equine Veterinary Journal*, Suppl 27 (Equine Clinical Behaviour), 44–8.

Dedication

Many thanks to all the people who kindly offered their horses to be part of this book. A further thanks to all of my teachers, including my parents, my animals, my friends and my family. I can never repay you for the knowledge and support you have given me over the years, but as a small gesture of thanks I dedicate this book to you.

Acknowledgements

First, I would like to thank Professor Daniel Mills for writing the foreword. I would also like to extend a big thank you to the following people for volunteering themselves and/or their horses to be part of this book:

Allie Samples
Emma Hennessey
Lesley Walker
Lucy Dentith
Lynne Chappell
Martin and Terri Shaw
Paula Mayne
Rachael Davies
Rachel Simmons
Ross and Melanie Barker of www.progressivehorse.co.uk
Shannon Bain.

Finally, I would like to thank my photographers:

Emily Smedley
Lynne Chappell
Paul Lethbridge.

Introduction:
From White Coats to Rosettes

Since the 1800s, scientists have been discovering how animals of many species both learn and adapt to their surroundings. The insights we now have into the mind of every species, including the horse, are astounding. The learning abilities and mechanisms of the mammalian brain are being documented in detail to the best of science's ability. This knowledge of learning has been applied thoroughly, in practical situations as well as in the laboratory, leading to the development of training theories which are both reliable and effective. This knowledge is used extensively, with great success, in the training of dogs and of animals in many of the world's zoos and sea life centres. In fact, today you would struggle to find a modern dog or animal training manual which doesn't use 'learning theory' as its basis. Learning theory has revolutionised not only the methods used to train dogs and other animals, but even the way *we* think about the way *they* think.

Horses actually learn in straightforward and predictable ways. This is why we can train and communicate with them so effectively; attempting to ride on the back of an animal with no predictability of behaviour would be a formidable task. Many would think of this view of horses as cold and simplistic. However, I do not think the removal of the anthropomorphic myths about horses is cold: it allows us to view the true nature of the horse. They are still beautiful, sentient and interesting creatures, who are prepared to be our companions. The only truth we have about the horse's mind and the way they learn is that which can be predictably tested and applied in training. It is this truth which allows us a deeper understanding of our equine friends and to forge a relationship with them.

Understanding these laws of learning can help horse owners and trainers work with their horses in a way that maintains the horse's welfare as paramount within a training programme. This is not because learning theory is inherently an ethical theory, but because knowledge of the theory can allow us to apply it to the horse in a way that makes it as easy as possible for the horse to understand and succeed during training. Furthermore, it allows us to avoid any behavioural side effects, such as fear or aggression, caused by the inappropriate application of training.

Why are these techniques and ideas not used as the basis of training in the horse world? The honest answer is, I don't know. Learning theory is as effective when applied to horses as it is to dogs and other animals. All training which is effective, from happy hacking to circus training or eventing to classical dressage, is so because the training has worked within the laws of learning theory. However, often trainers don't realise exactly why a training technique has been effective. A study by Warren-Smith and McGreevy (2008) found a lack of understanding of learning in horses, and the application of learning in training, by horse training coaches. It was found that 79.5% of the coaches thought positive reinforcement was 'very useful'; however, only 2.8% explained its use in horse training correctly. Interestingly, when the coaches were asked about the usefulness of negative reinforcement, only 19.3% of coaches considered it 'very useful', with only 11.9% correctly explaining its use. Punishment was considered 'very useful' by 5.2% of the coaches, although only 5.4% correctly explained punishment.

If a trainer applies a technique without true knowledge of why the technique works successfully the training cannot progress as quickly and mistakes or problems cannot be identified and corrected. This is exactly where a basic knowledge of learning theory can be critical to training. If a trainer knows why their training is effective, they can train faster, more ethically and more sympathetically and can analyse why any failures of training may occur – therefore having a much higher chance of correcting mistakes when they first appear rather than allowing training to break down.

Gradually, more of the horse world is embracing learning theory. Many new trainers use and teach learning theory and understand the many opportunities it can offer horse trainers of every discipline. Some horse training manuals now include chapters on learning theory. The aim of this book is to define learning theory and how to train using this knowledge, simply and clearly, to all people whether they are interested in riding, training, competing, solving behaviour problems or simply living a contented life with their horse.

Whether you are a happy hacker, a horse trainer or an international competitor, knowing how to apply learning theory is the key to all good training. Learning theory teaches us how the horse learns from his environment and then applies this knowledge to adapting most successfully to his environment. This understanding of equine learning can be applied very successfully during training to produce a happy and co-operative horse, who is involved in the training process rather than a victim of it. Whether you train using the principles of natural horsemanship or traditional horsemanship, or have simply learned to train horses through experience, every aspect of your training that succeeds will do so because it works with the horse's learning capabilities and thus within the theory of learning. Your training works for a reason and within this book is the theory behind that reason.

None of the ideas or methods in this book is my own. Learning theory is an established discipline developed over many years. What I wish to convey to you is its legacy and how to apply learning theory to everyday training situations. Not only for effective results, but results that are sympathetic to the horse as a sentient, intelligent being and which put the horse's welfare first. The purpose of this book is not to sell or publicise a particular method, but to communicate the principles of learning theory in an easy to understand way. These principles can be applied by the reader to teach the horse anything they desire or to solve any training problem they may encounter, in a range of different and effective ways. Knowing learning theory gives you many approaches to any one problem, whereas a single method alone gives only one answer to many problems.

Within this book you will find information on all the different areas of learning theory needed to train your horse. Furthermore, there are learning recaps which summarise the key ideas within each chapter, training guides and case studies to help you with your training, and training logs to record your progress.

The Principles of Good Horse Training

To begin this chapter, I feel it is necessary to answer two questions.

1. What is horse training?
2. What constitutes good horse training, as opposed to bad horse training?

To answer the first question, you are training your horse in every moment you spend around him. Every moment you spend in the presence of your horse, he is learning how to act and react around you. When the horse learns from the handler, the handler is training the horse. As horse handlers, we are a large and influential part of the horse's environment. We are training them whether this training is conscious or unconscious, because horses, like humans, learn from their environment every moment they are alive. Even when you are not specifically training the horse to do a task or to behave in a certain manner, your actions will be training your horse to behave in certain ways around you. We must always be aware of our actions around horses, in order that their training is consistent.

The second question could be said to be one which could only have a subjective answer; as such, this is my opinion as to what qualifies as 'good horse training'. There are many elements of horse training that could be mentioned here, but the following are the two that I feel are most important. Firstly, and of primary importance, good horse training should take into account the horse's welfare; as such it should be non-violent, cause as little stress or fear as possible and take into account that the horse is a sentient and intelligent animal. The only time I would advocate any striking of the horse is when the handler's physical well-being is in great danger and striking the horse is the only option at that point, i.e. another technique could not be used to remove the threat. Further to this, good horse training should be as effective at communicating the human's desires to the horse as possible. Good communication between horse and handler is required for truly excellent horse training. The creation of the communication channel is the sole responsibility of the handler; the horse cannot be blamed for misunderstanding the handler since he does not have the capacity to adapt intellectually as we do. The horse will react to the communication in the way he believes is best for his survival and comfort.

It is our duty as horse owners and trainers to train in a way that is both ethical (holds the horse's welfare as a primary concern) and effective. If a technique is more effective but requires that the horse's welfare is compromised, then another more ethically appropriate method should be found.

Obviously, if you find yourself faced with an emergency, it may be necessary to compromise immediate training for the horse's longer-term well-being. For example, if have to load a lorry-phobic horse into a horse lorry to go to the veterinary hospital, then it may be necessary to make a compromise in the method used to load the horse, in order to get the horse to hospital and ensure his long-term survival. However, in a non-emergency situation, welfare should always be paramount during training.

It is important to remember that no horse was born to be trained or ridden. Indeed, some horses may never wish to be ridden because of a physical issue or a psychological disposition brought on by experience of the human species. Horses by nature wish to live on grass plains, eat copious amounts of roughage and live in herds. For the horse to have contact with humans is something that, by nature, only humans desire. It is a hard truth that riding and training is something that as humans we force upon the horse. This does not, however, mean that horses cannot learn to find pleasure in their time spent with us humans, during both ground and ridden training, if the training is empathetic (takes into account how the horse feels about and reacts to its training) and is enjoyable for the horse. If you observe the equine species as being sentient and conscious, we owe it to them to allow their lives among humans to be enjoyable experiences, as free of pain and fear as possible, whilst also having an animal which is safe and co-operative. It is also worth noting that a horse which is contented in his training, both on the ground and whilst ridden, is a much safer animal than one who is stressed by it or fearful of it.

In my opinion there are ten principles which underlie all good horse training. These principles are not restricted to horse training but apply to the training of any animal. These principles will not be revelations to anyone who has been working with the wonderful species *Equus caballus*, but they are important factors to consider if one wants to become a good and fair horse trainer. Furthermore, they are also often neglected in the pursuit of an end result that we feel is necessary for the horse.

TEN BASIC PRINCIPLES OF GOOD HORSEMANSHIP

There is no magic recipe to being a good horse trainer. Most people can learn to be brilliant horse trainers with a knowledge of learning theory and by following a few simple principles which ensure a good horse/handler relationship and good communication.

1. Always Be Patient

To be a good horse trainer you must be very patient, both with the horse and with yourself. Frustration over the horse's behaviour or training will only result in the training becoming negatively affected. During training, an inner sense of calm is always necessary, even if the training is not going as well as desired. If you are patient with the horse he will get to the end result eventually. However, if you lose patience with the horse, the relationship and trust between the horse and handler will be diminished.

2. Have Empathy for the Horse

Have empathy for the horse, try to understand how he views and feels about the training. Try imagining yourself in the horse's shoes – would you understand or enjoy the training? As humans, we have a list or picture of what we want from the horse, but the horse does not have this knowledge unless he is trained in a clear manner. When training the horse, ask yourself whether you would under- stand what was being ask of you, if you didn't know the expected outcome of the training. The horse will rarely misbehave if he truly knows what is desired of him, and as long as what is being asked of him is considered to be safe and beneficial to his survival. Good training will ensure that the horse co-operates with the handler because the horse considers it to be beneficial and safe to do so. If the horse isn't doing as asked, put yourself in the horse's place. Is the horse frightened or confused by the handler or its environment? Or has he simply not been given enough time to learn what is desired of him? If he doesn't understand what is being asked of him, then try to find a different way to ask, rather than just asking louder or applying more pressure, which is the equivalent of shouting at a foreign person in English. Being able to see the training from the perspective of the horse allows us not only to forge a better relationship with him, but also to understand why he behaves as he does.

3. Physical Violence and Excessive Force Should Never be Used!

There is never any excuse to use physical violence, or excessive force, to get the horse to comply with the demands of humans unless, as I stated earlier, you are in grave danger and have no other option available to you. However, other than in these very rare events, the means never justify the ends if training techniques that use fear and/or pain have been utilised in the horse's training. No result is so important that it justifies violence or excessive force in horse training, and thus compromises the horse's welfare and well-being. There are effective ways of dealing with unwanted behaviour from the horse without resorting to violence, as will be described in detail in Chapter 10.

There are only three results that occur when a horse is treated with brutality:

- the horse breaks down and becomes robotic as he learns that he is helpless
- the horse will retaliate with extremes of aggression
- the horse becomes fearful and flighty.

None of these results will develop a relationship between horse and handler that is based on mutual trust, pleasure and co-operation. No part of training should be physically or mentally damaging to the horse. A horse that works out of fear of consequences is not a willing partner, but a slave.

4.   Know When to Walk Away and When Not to Train At All

If you feel sad, angry or frustrated, either before or during training, be aware that these feelings can often cloud your judgement and reactions to the horse, so that mistakes are made and training is impeded. It is not a failure but rather a display of intellect, clarity of judgement and knowledge of ourselves to walk away until we have regained a clear, calm and focused mind. Negative emotions will do nothing other than have a negative effect on training. If you train professionally, be aware that learning to focus your mind and thoughts and clear away negative emotions, despite the day's occurrences, so that you are focused on the horse and your success as a partnership only, can greatly improve your experience of training and thus your results from training.

5.   Don't Panic – We All Make Mistakes

Remember that no one is perfect and that during training we will all make mistakes, especially when using a technique which is perhaps unfamiliar. As long as the horse's welfare is always the top priority, a mistake in training should have limited negative consequences. So merely analyse where you went wrong and work on changing it into a success. Learning theory is a toolbox and we all pick the wrong tool to use on occasion. Don't be afraid to stop, analyse where you went wrong and start again, maybe with a different tool. This is a more sensible and effective way to train, rather than persisting with a technique and possibly training the wrong behaviour or compromising the horse's welfare. Dwelling on a mistake will not undo what has been done, but it may prevent you from enjoying your training and progressing with your horse. Learning from what went wrong can be a valuable learning tool and will make you a better trainer in the end.

6.   There are No Bad Students, Only Bad Teachers

During training, if something is not going how you expected, remember to analyse your training first and foremost. Good trainers will always look at themselves before the horse, if they are not progressing as they would like. Most problems during training are caused by the handler, rather than the horse. Good teachers amend their teaching technique to suit the student as an individual. The trainer should acknowledge that every horse has his own abilities and talents. It is the trainer's job to find the best technique to train the horse, rather than to blame the horse for their own mistakes. Furthermore, if a mistake is made during training, the quicker the trainer realises their mistake, rather than blaming the horse, the faster it can be corrected, ensuring the training remains productive and enjoyable.

7. Why Won't My Horse . . . ?

There are three potential factors which prevent a horse from complying with the wishes of a human.

* **The horse doesn't understand what is being asked of him.** This is a very common cause of problems during the training and keeping of a horse. The needs of the human are not communicated to the horse in a way that the horse can understand and therefore confusion and frustration ensue. Never simply use more pressure or ask louder if the horse seems not to understand. Again, this is equivalent to shouting at a foreign person in English. Rather, find a different way to communicate to the horse what you require from him.
* **The horse can't do it.** If a horse is in pain or suffers from an ailment which prevents him from performing the wish of the human, it is likely that the horse will attempt not to perform the behaviour and if pushed to perform, may become helpless, aggressive or flighty. If the horse is not progressing with his training, ask yourself if it is possible that there is some physical issue which prevents him from doing so. It can be a very effective indicator of a physical issue within the horse if, as a trainer, you listen to the horse rather than blindly insisting.
* **It is more beneficial for the horse not to comply.** If the horse is rewarded by not complying with the human, or indeed escapes doing something he feels is scary or not beneficial to his survival, it is likely that the horse will attempt not to comply with the demands of the human. For example, if the horse runs away from the human who wants to catch him, he may avoid being stabled, handled and/or ridden. It is part of training to make it

more beneficial for the horse to comply with the demands of the human than to not comply.

Horses do not resist complying with humans' demands because of spite, revenge, 'taking the mickey' or to purposelessly defy the handler. These are afflictions of the human mind, which it is highly unlikely that the horse possesses, since they require elements of higher cognition not available to the equine species. That is not to say that the horse might not go against the handler's wishes; it simply means that he does it because he is fearful or because previous experience has caused him to believe that his behaviour is the best way to survive in his environment.

8.   Remember It's Supposed to be Fun

Although the end result of training is important, the journey to the end result is just as important. Allow yourself the time and clarity of mind to train in the here and now, rather than focusing entirely on the end result. This will ensure that you can progress without pressure, frustration or stress and it is likely that you will progress faster and enjoy your training. It will also mean that, as a trainer, you are less likely to cut corners or sacrifice the horse's welfare during training. Never allow others to enforce a timetable on your training and remain strong if faced with peer pressure to push your horse. It is unknown whether or not horses have a sense of fun, although many trainers would anecdotally say they do. They do play with each other and occasionally with humans, so it may be possible that they do. However, it is possible to tell whether the horse finds training rewarding, and is relaxed and content during training. You should always aim for your horse to engage with you during training and find training rewarding, so that the horse desires to be with the handler and be trained.

9.   Every Horse is an Individual and Should be Treated as Such

Every horse you keep, train and ride will be an individual, with his own innate and learned traits of character. Be flexible enough in your approach to training to tailor it to best fit the horse as an individual.

Where training is concerned, one size does not fit all. It is important to know the core principles of training so that no one method is followed absolutely but rather the principles are applied to the individual horse in a way which is most effective.

10. Always Put the Horse First

With the right handling, a horse can be more than a tool for riding or competition; he can also be a true companion and a partner in any activity. The horse is an intelligent creature, capable of physical feeling and experiencing at least basic emotions, and should be treated as such during training. The horse's welfare should be the primary concern of any trainer. It should also be the endeavour of the trainer to make training enjoyable for the horse. The horse should co-operate with the trainer out of choice, not force. Never sacrifice the trust of the horse or his welfare to gain a quick result or the approval of peers or experts. Partnership between horse and handler should be based on training which is productive, consistent and pleasurable for all involved.

These principles should be maintained regardless of what technique within learning theory you employ to train your horse. The rest of this book is dedicated to explaining how horses learn and how to apply this knowledge to ensure your training is most productive and enjoyable.

LEARNING RECAP

The 10 Principles of Good Horse Training

1. Always be patient.
2. Have empathy for the horse.
3. Physical violence and excessive force should never be used!
4. Know when to walk away and when not to train at all.
5. Don't panic – we all make mistakes.
6. There are no bad students, only bad teachers.
7. Why won't my horse . . . ? Ask yourself:
   - Is the horse confused?
   - Can the horse do what is wanted?
   - Is it more beneficial for the horse not to comply or does he believe that complying would be dangerous?
8. Remember it's supposed to be fun.
9. Every horse is an individual and should be treated as such.
10. Always put the horse first.

Does Classical Conditioning Ring a Bell?

Classical conditioning was one of the first concepts of learning and one that can be observed in species from flies and snails to horses and humans. Classical conditioning is simply the formation of an association between two stimuli. Classical conditioning can be commonly observed in horses; for example, we all know of horses who don't like their owners to catch them in the field because they associate being caught with being stabled or being worked unpleasantly, or horses who won't stand for the farrier because they associate being shod with unpleasant experiences.

An Accidental Discovery

The journey of learning theory began in the laboratory of Ivan Petrovich Pavlov in 1920s Russia. Pavlov had abandoned his religious career, following in the footsteps of his father, Peter Dmitrievich Pavlov, and pursued his passion for science. At this time Pavlov was not investigating learning at all; he was interested in physiology and the functioning of the digestive glands. Pavlov's investigation of these glands consisted of presenting dogs with appetizing food and measuring how much drool they produced, known as the salivary response. Before the food was presented to the dogs, a bell was rung signalling 'food time'.

Part way through the experiment, Pavlov, being an observant sort of person, realised that the dogs were now drooling at the sound of the bell and not, as they had done previously, when the food arrived. The dogs had learnt that the sound of the bell predicted the imminent arrival of tasty food. The association between the sound of the bell and the arrival of the food had caused the dogs to drool at the sound of the bell, although a bell in normal circumstances would never illicit such a response in a dog. Effectively, Pavlov had trained his dogs to drool at the sound of the bell. This is classical conditioning at work. In layman's terms, this effect is known as anticipation.

As mentioned before, classical conditioning is the **formation of an association between two stimuli**. In order for classical conditioning to occur, the two stimuli must happen close together in both time and space. This ensures that an association can be easily formed between them. If there is a large amount of time or space between the two stimuli, either the association may take a long time to form or an undesirable association may arise. This is the most important factor to take into account when undertaking classical conditioning training.

Definition: A stimulus is any event or object which effectively activates the sensory apparatus of a living organism, potentially involving both the internal and external environments of the body.

Usually a stimulus becomes associated with another stimulus that is significantly pleasant or unpleasant, initiating a behavioural response. If the two stimuli are paired with sufficient regularity, the original stimulus becomes conditioned and will elicit the behavioural response without the presence of the pairing stimulus. In the case of Pavlov's dogs, the original stimulus was the sound of the bell. This was paired with the arrival of food, which was very pleasant for the dogs. After many days of this routine the sound of the bell became a conditioned stimulus, so that the bell's sound would now elicit the drooling response in the dog as a conditioned (learned) response.

For example, horses often act excitedly by banging their stable door, nickering or head shaking when their owners enter the feed room of the yard. Although the feed room has no intrinsic value to the horse (unconditioned stimulus), it has learnt by repetition that the owner entering the feed room predicts the imminent arrival of food. The feed room has become a conditioned stimulus and the horse has learned that the owner entering the feed room means that he is about to be fed. Therefore, the horse now becomes excited when the owner enters the feed room.

DIFFERENT STIMULI AND RESPONSE TERMS

There are two types of stimuli which can be presented to the horse. Some stimuli a horse will react to without any conditioning because they are intrinsically important to the horse. Stimuli that horses react to innately or instinctually are know as 'primary' or 'unconditioned (US)' stimuli. Some stimuli that usually hold value for the horse, without any learning being required, include food, social contact, loud noises and water. Horses don't need to learn that food is pleasant, because it intrinsically tastes good and satisfies the horse's innate hunger drive.

Horses, being flight animals, tend to have a slightly fearful curiosity about new stimuli, so more objects tend to hold negative meaning for them than for other species, such as dogs. For example, for many horses road signs, clippers and plastic bags will be counted as fearful stimuli, despite no previous negative experiences of the items. These items are innately scary to the horse because he is programmed to be somewhat scared of new stimuli. The horse's personality will also determine how fearful, or not, he is of novel objects.

Stimuli that horses only react to after conditioning has taken place, and the horse has learnt the meaning of the stimulus, are known as 'secondary' or 'conditioned (CS)' stimuli. These stimuli consist of most objects regularly observed in the horse's environment. Such objects will only elicit a response after conditioning has taken place. Once the horse has learnt to associate a meaning with the stimulus, it becomes a 'conditioned' stimulus.

An unlearnt reaction to a stimulus, i.e. one that occurs naturally, is known as an 'unconditioned response (UR)'. Horses have these unconditioned responses because, by responding innately to the presence of food, loud noises and flapping branches, the horse has managed to ensure his survival in the wild. When horses used to live in their natural wild habitat, those that didn't respond quickly to these stimuli ended up dead very quickly. These responses have evolved to occur naturally and do not have to be learnt by repetition; you only get one chance to run away from the tiger. Interestingly, loud noises and flapping branches are not usually life threatening, especially as there are now very few tigers roaming modern-day Britain, and therefore the responses are a waste of the horse's energy. It is also worth noting that a horse's personality can affect his innate reactions; some horses are naturally more responsive than others.

Alternatively, a 'conditioned response (CR)' to a stimulus is one that has to be learnt. When a young horse is being taught to have his hooves picked out, he will not automatically know to lift his hoof when asked by a pull on the fetlock. This behaviour has to be learnt (conditioned). Picking up a hoof is a conditioned response.

Don't be put off by all the scientific terms. Consider the following practical example.

Little Albert

In the 1920s Watson and Rayner carried out one of the first conditioning experiments by teaching an 11-month-old child named Albert to become fearful of a white rat. Albert initially showed absolutely no fear of the little white rat and to demonstrate this he was allowed to play with the animal at the beginning of the experiment. The white rat was a 'neutral stimulus (NS)' to Little Albert. The experimenters did know, however, that Albert was afraid of loud noises, an 'unconditioned response (UR)'. During the experiment, in order to condition Albert to fear the rat, the experimenters would make a loud noise by striking a large steel pipe with a hammer, just above and behind Albert's head, whilst he was playing with the rat (luckily experimenters are no longer allowed to scare babies in their experiments). The loud noise would scare Albert, who would cry and the rat was then taken away. Only seven paired presentations of the rat and the loud noise were required before Little Albert began to cry and struggle on sight of the rat, despite the absence of the loud noise. The crying and struggling was a conditioned response (CR) to the presence of the rat, which had become a conditioned stimulus (CS). Little Albert had formed an association between the rat and the presence of a fearful event. A brilliant, if mean, demonstration of the effectiveness of conditioning.

> **Training Task: How to Classically Condition Your Horse**
>
> Knowing how to use classical conditioning can be invaluable in training your horse. Conditioning your horse is very simple and can be very useful for encouraging a horse to react in a certain way to certain objects and/or events. If you wish your horse to enjoy an event, to like an object or to not fear a scary object, then make sure he associates that event or object with something pleasant.

SPECIFIC TRAINING SITUATIONS

Foals and Farriers

Teaching foals to get used to the sights and smells of the farrier is a necessary task, if the foal is to grow up to be an easy-to-handle and relaxed adult. For young horses that have had little or no experience of the farrier, the smell of the smoke and the sound of the hammer on the anvil can be a scary experience. To ensure the foal doesn't develop a fear of the farrier, make sure that the situation is associated with a very pleasant experience for the foal. Feeding the foal near to the farrier, whilst he is working, will cause the foal to associate the farrier with a pleasant experience, i.e. being fed. The foal will become conditioned to enjoy the farrier's visits and will be easier to introduce to trimming at the appropriate time. A very simple but important life lesson. This can also be done with a horse that has learned to fear the farrier.

No More Standing in the Rain

Even the trickiest to catch horse can be conditioned to come in without fuss by feeding him a few treats in a bucket once he comes in. Consistently giving the horse a few treats for being caught causes him to associate coming in with a pleasant experience; therefore he will learn that coming in is a nice event and not something to avoid.

Horses That Don't Like Men or Women

Some horses who have had bad experiences of one or other sex develop a fear of that gender. It is very possible that horses manage to discriminate the gender of a person on the basis of smell. Horses have an amazing sense of smell and human sex hormones and pheromones are very distinctive, so it is likely that horses can distinguish between men and women. To tackle the issue of horses that are afraid of one or other sex, it is a good idea to always get a member of that sex to feed the horse his dinner. Alternatively, if your horse particularly enjoys being groomed, scratched or massaged, get a member of the sex he doesn't like to spend time with him performing these activities. By associating the sex of human he doesn't like with nice experiences, he will be conditioned to realise that they are not so bad after all.

These are just a few examples of the endless list of situations in which classical conditioning can be applied with great success. The rest is up to you.

LEARNING RECAP

Reiterating the key points of the chapter and most important concepts to understand, to make your training as successful as possible.

Key Terms	Recap of Definition and Important Concepts
Classical conditioning	Formation of an association between two stimuli, such as associating the handler with pleasurable experiences, will encourage the horse to want to associate with the handler. This association can be a pleasurable association (as before) or disagreeable. These associations will affect the horse's behaviour.
Unconditioned responses (UR)	A response to a stimulus, which the horse has not learnt, but occurs innately i.e. fear of loud noises.
Conditioned responses (US)	A response to a stimulus which has been learned, e.g. fearing electric fencing due to being shocked.
Neutral stimulus (NS)	A stimulus that has no preconditioned meaning for the horse.
Conditioned stimulus (CS)	A stimulus that has been conditioned to have meaning for the horse, e.g. the horse seeing his feed bowl and knowing that means the arrival of food, or a horse that fears a stick due to it having been used inappropriately on him in the past.

MY TRAINING LOG

Here is a place to record your classical conditioning training experiences and observations. Any notes which might help your future training, or your horse as an individual, can also be written down to help you. The skills you will need to condition will be individual to your horse and his likes and dislikes. If you have more than one horse or wish to use the table in the future, it can be scanned and printed out, or you can make your own.

Skill To Be Conditioned	Date Started	Notes	Date Finished

Knowing Your Horse: A Guide to Equine Learning, Training and Behaviour
Emma Lethbridge
9781405191647

Living with the Consequences

Animals, including horses and humans, navigate their environment through learning from the consequences of their actions. Learning from the consequences of his actions allows the horse to perform the behaviours that are most beneficial to him, more often, and conversely, to avoid those that are detrimental to him. This ensures that the horse has the best chance of survival in his environment.

A simple example of such learning is when horses first meet electric fencing. Usually the horse will sniff the fencing and as a consequence get a sharp shock on the nose. The horse therefore learns that he must not touch the electric fencing. Horses are very good at first trial learning from negative consequences. Being a prey animal in his natural habitat, the horse would have to learn to avoid negative experiences quickly. If the horse didn't learn to avoid food that made him feel ill and to fear strangely rustling bushes, he wouldn't survive. Horses also learn quickly from positive consequences to their behaviour.

OPERANT CONDITIONING

Learning through the consequences of behaviour is known as 'operant conditioning'. Horses have the ability to learn both highly desirable and undesirable behaviours in their domestic environments through operant conditioning. The following example demonstrates the amazing ability of the horse to learn about and manipulate his environment.

Clever Hans, the Counting Horse

Clever Hans lived at the turn of the 20th century. Mr Von Osten, Hans' owner, claimed to have taught Hans many intellectual tasks, including how to add, subtract, multiply, divide, tell the time, read and spell, among other things. This attracted the attention of the media and Hans became popular with the Victorians, especially with the interest in animal intelligence being spurred on by the publication of Charles Darwin's work on animals and species. Von Osten would ask Hans questions during the show and Hans would answer by tapping his hoof on the floor.

Hans' intellectual abilities were investigated in 1904 by a commission of 13 professionals and it was concluded that there were no tricks involved in Hans training and at this point the study of Hans' speculated abilities was transferred to a psychologist called Oskar Pfungst. Pfungst studied the horse's responses by using different questioners, isolating Hans from the audience and the owner during testing, and testing him when the owner didn't know the answers to the questions. Pfungst found that Hans could get the right answer regardless of who asked the questions, with a response rate of 89% if he could see Van Osten. However, if Hans could not see Van Osten his correct response rate fell to 6%. With further investigation, Pfungst found that Hans could not actually perform the intellectual tasks but was taking minute changes in Van Osten's tension, posture and expression as tiny cues as to when to stop tapping.

Hans was able to pick up on cues so small that the audiences and even the commission of 13 professionals could not work out how he was able to perform the sums correctly. This talent is not just limited to Hans. Pfungst found in following studies that 90% of horses were able to respond to cues so tiny that they are subconscious to most humans in both performance and observation.

The study of Hans shows us just how careful we have to be when we train our horses as they are able to learn from tiny cues and consequences in their environment. We must always be aware of how we may be affecting our horse's behaviour.

Operant conditioning forms an association between behaviour and consequence. An operant is simply an action by an organism which results in an outcome. It is this outcome of the operant (the behaviour) which will determine whether the behaviour is performed again and with what regularity. Through the consequence, the horse learns to repeat the behaviour, or not; he has therefore become conditioned.

The Puzzling Cat

In the late 1800s an American scientist called Edward Lee Thorndike was studying learning in animals. Thorndike's experiment consisted of creating puzzle boxes for cats, with a lever escape mechanism, which could be pressed for immediate escape. Thorndike found that when the cat was placed inside the box, he would thrash wildly until the lever was pressed and the cat escaped. Escaping was desirable to the cat, so over a period of many trials the cat learned exactly which behaviour allowed him to escape, i.e. the pressing of the lever. The cat had associated the pressing behaviour with a desirable consequence, i.e. escaping from the box. After many studies of this kind, in 1898 Thorndike concluded his work by formulating the Law of Effect.

The Law of Effect

The simple version of Thorndike's law states that:

'If the consequence of a response is undesirable, that behavioural response will decrease. If the consequence of a behaviour is desirable, the animal will increase in its repetition of that response'.

A simple flow diagram of this behavioural association can be modelled as:

Stimulus → Response → Consequence → Implication

In the case of Thorndike's cats the diagram would go like this.

Stimulus – Cat placed into puzzle box.

↓

Response – Cat eventually pushes lever and activates escape mechanism.

↓

Consequence – Cat escapes the box which is desirable to the cat, who does not like being in the box.

↓

Implication – Cat pushes the lever more quickly next time he is placed in the puzzle box.

A Working Example

Stimulus – Horse asked for a schooling movement.

↓

Response – Good schooling movement performed by the horse.

↓

Consequence – Horse given scratch and long rein which he enjoys, and as such is desirable to him.

↓

Implication – Good schooling movement more likely to be repeated.

Or in the case of the mugging horse:

Stimulus – Owner with food in pockets.

↓

Response – Horse aggressively mugs the owner's pockets.

↓

Consequence – Eventually the owner gives in and gives the horse a treat.

↓

Implication – More persistent mugging next time.

APPLYING SIMPLE OPERANT CONDITIONING

Applying operant conditioning is really very easy. If you like your horse's behaviour, i.e. when he stands nicely at the mounting block, give this behaviour a desirable consequence for the horse, i.e. give him a scratch or a treat. However, if you don't like a behaviour, for example, if your horse is kicking his door for attention, give this behavioural response an undesirable consequence, e.g. don't give him attention or attach a bit of rubber matting in front of the door so that kicking it causes it to swing back and forth; an undesirable (but not painful) consequence to the kicking behaviour. If the behaviour no longer brings a desirable consequence, it will decrease in frequency.

Training Task: 'Don't Mug Me' Training

Hold the treat in your hand. The horse will most likely try and snatch the treat from you (known as 'mugging'). Ignore this behaviour, whilst keeping your hand safe. As soon as the horse looks away, extend your hand to the horse and give him the treat. Repeat this exercise, until the horse learns that in order to get the treat he must not mug your pockets. Once you have taught the horse this exercise, make sure that you never reward the mugging behaviour in the future. This will prevent the horse mugging you for treats.

The following photo sequence shows Shannon teaching Remmy not to mug her, but to receive his reward in a calm and safe manner. This training is done under strict supervision and Remmy has already done this training with an adult trainer. You may find that horses and ponies may have to be reminded of the no mugging rule with different handlers, especially with children, or with anyone who has previously rewarded them for the mugging behaviour. However, children are capable of following and applying this rule as Shannon (age 12) demonstrates. Figure 3.1 shows Remmy trying to get the treat from Shannon's hand. Shannon doesn't give Remmy the reward until he stands quietly and looks away from her (Fig. 3.2). Once Remmy is standing at a safe distance and looking away from the reward, Shannon rewards him at a suitably safe distance from her (Fig. 3.3). Shannon is conditioning Remmy using positive reinforcement conditioning to receive a reward in a safe manner.

Figure 3.1   Remmy trying to mug Shannon.

Figure 3.2   Remmy looking away politely.

Figure 3.3   Remmy receiving his reward at a polite distance from Shannon.

LEARNING RECAP

Reiterating the key points of this chapter and the important concepts to understand to make your training as successful as possible.

Key Terms	Recap of Definition and Important Concepts
Operant conditioning	Learning through the consequences of behaviour. Operant conditioning forms an association between behaviour and consequence, which has an implication for the future production of that behaviour by the animal.
Thorndike's Law of Effect	Defines the implication of the consequence of the behaviour. The Law of Effect states that if the consequence of a response is undesirable, that behavioural response will decrease. If the consequence of a behaviour is desirable, the animal will increase in its repetition of that response

MY TRAINING LOG

Here is a place to record your training, experiences and observations relating to the important 'don't mug me' task learned in this chapter.

Skill Trained	Date Started	Notes	Date Finished
'Don't mug me' training			

Knowing Your Horse: A Guide to Equine Learning, Training and Behaviour
Emma Lethbridge
9781405191647

All Possible Consequences

It may seem impossible to predict all the possible consequences of a behaviour. How can we use operant conditioning to train with so many possible consequences? Thankfully, a very clever scientist called B.F. Skinner found that these consequences fit conveniently into four simple categories. The four possible consequences to any behaviour are as follows.

1. Something Good can start or be presented ... **Positive Reinforcement**
2. Something Good can end or be taken away ... **Negative Punishment**
3. Something Bad can start or be presented ... **Positive Punishment**
4. Something Bad can end or be taken away ... **Negative Reinforcement**

Understanding these four categories means that we can fully comprehend how a horse is conditioned to behave in a certain manner by his environment and/or by his trainer, and in fact how horses condition their owners.

DEFINING POSITIVE AND NEGATIVE CONSEQUENCES

When talking about learning, positive and negative have slightly different meanings than when used in everyday speech. During a positive consequence something is added to the learning environment. The thing that is added can be something good or bad; for example, food can be added to the environment which would be pleasurable for the horse, but a loud scary noise could also be added to the environment, which would be an undesirable consequence for the horse. Both of these consequences would be considered positive because both were added to the learning environment as the consequence of a behaviour.

Conversely, a negative consequence refers to when something is removed from the learning environment as a consequence of a behaviour. Again, the thing that is removed can be good or bad. For example, if food is removed from the horse as a consequence of an unwanted behaviour, this would be a undesirable consequence for the horse; however, if discomfort is removed from the horse's environment this would be a desirable consequence for the horse. In both these examples either an object or experience is removed from the horse's environment, as a consequence of the production of a behaviour. These consequences are both defined as negative because of the removal element of the consequences. But the removal can be perceived as desirable or undesirable for the horse, depending on the stimulus removed.

Tip

An easy way to remember the difference between positive and negative consequences.

A **Positive (+)** consequence = something being **Added (+)** to the environment.
A **Negative (−)** consequence = something being **Removed (−)** from the learning environment.

Distinguishing between positive and negative consequences is important for identifying what type of event is conditioning the horse's behaviour and also in order to clearly define how we are training the horse by providing consequences to his behaviour. These individual positive and negative consequences that can be used in training will be discussed in more detail later in the book in Chapters 6–9.

The next part of the chapter will simply outline each form of learning so that the basic definition of each form is easy to understand and can be built upon in later chapters.

REINFORCEMENT

Reinforcement is defined as any consequence to a behaviour which makes that behaviour more likely to occur. When a behaviour occurs more often due to reinforcement, that behaviour is said to have been strengthened. Reinforcement can be positive or negative.

Positive Reinforcement – The Power of Pleasure

Positive reinforcement is the adding of a pleasurable stimulus to the horse's learning environment as a consequence of a behaviour, encouraging that behaviour to occur more often in the future.

Positive reinforcers are anything that your horse finds pleasurable, that can be presented to him when a behaviour occurs. For example, edible treats are a very strong positive reinforcer for most horses. Gentle scratches can also be used as an effective positive reinforcer; most horses have a place they really like to be scratched, usually around the neck/wither area, although make sure your horse really enjoys being scratched before trying to use scratching as a positive reinforcer, or it may have the opposite effect to the one desired. Other things such as turning the horse loose or allowing access to a favoured object can also be used as positive reinforcers, although these are practically more difficult to utilise, i.e. it is only really possible to turn a horse out once per training session without a lot of time and effort spent bringing him in from the field and turning him out for each occurrence of the behaviour, whereas food treats can be presented quickly and repeatedly, allowing much more training to be achieved per session.

The motivational power and learning potential of positive reinforcement is often underestimated. Just as humans will work hard for rewards, so will horses. Imagine if you had two bosses, one who offers you small rewards for your hard work, such as time off, while the other offers no reward and merely reprimands you for any incorrect work. Which boss would you rather work for? Also, your relationship with the first boss is likely to be better, as you associate him with nice things.

Similarly to classical conditioning, positive reinforcers will usually be more effective, and therefore have greater strengthening effect, the more essential they are to the horse's survival and well-being. Those reinforcers which are elements necessary for the horse's survival are known as primary reinforcers, so food is a very strong primary positive reinforcer for most horses. Pleasurable social contact and other pleasurable experiences will also have a strengthening effect on behaviour, but often this is less pronounced because they are not strictly necessary for the horse's survival. These reinforcers are known as secondary reinforcers.

Tip

It is important to note that all horses are individuals and as such they will have different reactions to positive reinforcers. Some horses (and especially ponies) will do anything desired for one pony nut; however, other horses may have little or no interest in food and may find a nice scratch or being let loose more pleasurable. It is important to know your horse and his likes and dislikes, so that you can organise his training to be most effective. Using food treats to train a horse who is not overly concerned with treats, but loves to be scratched, can be less effective than using scratches. If your horse is not motivated by one reward, try different types of rewards to see what works for him as an individual. If your horse is not motivated by any form of positive reinforcement, try looking into other forms of training which may suit your horse.

Negative Reinforcement – Escaping the Unpleasant

Negative reinforcement is simply the removing of an unpleasant stimulus in consequence of a behaviour. For example, when leading the horse, if he starts pulling towards a tasty-looking morsel of grass, pressure will be put on the halter, an unpleasant stimulus. When the horse changes his behaviour and stops pulling and begins following the owner, the pressure will be released, removing the unpleasant stimulus. The horse learns that by following the owner he can release the pressure on the halter.

In human terms, negative reinforcement occurs when you hit the snooze button on your alarm. The behaviour of hitting the snooze button gets rid of the aversive beeping noise, while escaping the horrid noise of the alarm reinforces the behaviour of hitting the snooze button.

Conditioners which can be used for negative reinforcement are anything which is unpleasant to the horse, i.e. discomfort or pressure. Negative reinforcement is sometimes used accidentally during riding. Although the reins, legs and seat should only be used as communicative cues to the horse during riding (the aids of riding should simply inform the horse as to what to do next), often they are used as negative reinforcement. For example, often riders will hold a contact on the reins until the horse stops and then release the contact. This is an example of negative reinforcement; the holding of the reins is uncomfortable for the horse but when he stops and the reins are released, he has escaped the unpleasant stimulus, reinforcing the stopping behaviour.

Tip

Negative reinforcement is not punishment – the two are very different! Negative reinforcement causes a behaviour to become strengthened (occur more often), whereas punishment causes a behaviour to become weakened (occur less often).

Now for a tricky bit. Negative reinforcement can actually be divided into two forms of learning; escape and avoidance learning. Escape learning occurs when the animal escapes an aversive stimulus by performing a behaviour. This behaviour is the one described above when the human escapes the nasty sound of the alarm clock by pressing the snooze button. However, escape learning can turn into avoidance learning: waking up just before the alarm sounds and turning it off can save the human listening to the horrible noise of the alarm, thus avoiding it.

Similarly, a horse may learn to remove the pressure from the head collar by moving closer to the owner when pressure is applied, thus escaping from the pressure. However, eventually it is hoped that he will learn not to pull on the head collar or lunge in the direction of every tasty morsel of grass, in order to avoid pressure being put on the head collar.

PUNISHMENT

Punishment is any consequence to a behaviour which results in that behaviour being less likely to occur in the future. When a behaviour occurs less often because of punishment, it is said that that behaviour has become weakened.

Positive Punishment

Positive punishment is the addition of an adverse stimulus as a consequence of a behaviour. The addition of an unpleasant stimulus discourages the behaviour from occurring in the future because it is undesirable for the horse. Positive punishment is used substantially in the horse world. Whips, spurs, kicking, smacking, rein pulling and shouting can all be examples of positive punishment. Whether they should be used, and their effect on the horse, is a long debate and will be discussed in detail in Chapter 9.

Negative Punishment

Negative punishment is the removal of something good as a consequence of a behaviour. The loss of a desired resource discourages the behaviour from reoccurring. It is difficult to apply negative punishment effectively to horses, although on occasion it can be useful. Humans learn well from negative punishment; many of us remember losing privileges (TV time or going out) or belongings being confiscated due to bad behaviour as children. All of these are forms of negative punishment; things that were desirable to us were removed as a consequence of a behaviour.

Stimuli which are pleasant to the horse and which can be removed easily can be used as conditioners for negative punishment; feed, attention, pleasurable contact, e.g. scratches, can all be used. Many horses like attention and some even will nip or head bash their owner for attention. One good example of negative punishment is for horses which are overly enthusiastic in their search for attention. In order to stop the nipping/head-bashing behaviour, remove your attention when the behaviour starts, i.e. walk away from the horse. The horse will associate the removal of your attention with his behaviour, an undesirable consequence. The key to making this technique work is being sure that the cause of the behaviour is the horse seeking your attention, and removing the attention completely as soon as the behaviour starts, i.e. not looking at or talking to the horse. Return to the horse when he is calm.

WHICH CONSEQUENCE?

Figure 4.1 represents a good way to remember the different consequences and how they change behaviour.

   If you are having difficulty figuring out exactly which consequence is governing your horse's behaviour, ask yourself the following questions.

1. **What is the behaviour that is being changed?** Identifying the exact behaviour to be adapted can be very useful in focusing your work. Often many behaviours can appear as one behaviour and sometimes it is necessary to analyse each behaviour in detail and work with each one individually.
2. **Is the behaviour being strengthened (occurring more often) or weakened (occurring less often)?**
3. **What was the consequence of the horse's behaviour?** Observe the immediate consequence of the horse's behaviour.
4. **Was the consequence an addition to the horse's environment or a removal?**

	Reinforcement	Punishment
Positive	Positive **Reinforcement** The addition of a pleasant stimulus.	Positive **Punishment** The addition of an unpleasant stimulus.
Negative	Negative **Reinforcement** The removal of an unpleasant stimulus.	Negative **Punishment** The removal of a pleasant stimulus.

Figure 4.1   The four possible consequences of a behaviour.

These questions can be invaluable in identifying the true adapting force shaping your horse's behaviour. The box below contains some examples.

Example A

1. What is the behaviour that is being changed? The horse standing still at the mounting block.
2. Is the behaviour being strengthened (occurring more often) or weakened (occurring less often)? Strengthened
3. What is the consequence to the horse's behaviour? Scratch on the neck (which the horse enjoys) for standing still.
4. Was the consequence an addition to the horse environment or a removal? An addition (the commencement of scratches).

This horse behaviour is being changed by **Positive Reinforcement**.

Example B

1. What is the behaviour that is being changed? The horse standing still at the mounting block.
2. Is the behaviour being strengthened (occurring more often) or weakened (occurring less often)? Weakened
3. What is the consequence to the horse's behaviour? Rider lands heavily in the saddle.
4. Was the consequence an addition to the horse environment or a removal? An addition (the uncomfortable landing of the rider).

This horse behaviour is being changed by **Positive Punishment**.

Example C

1. What is the behaviour that is being changed? The horse standing still at the mounting block.

2. Is the behaviour being strengthened (occurring more often) or weakened (occurring less often)? Weakened
3. What is the consequence to the horse's behaviour? When he gets on, the rider stops feeding the treats he gives the horse when on the mounting block.
4. Was the consequence an addition to the horse environment or a removal? A removal (the cessation of treat feeding).

The horse's behaviour is being changed by **Negative Punishment**.

Example D

1. What is the behaviour that is being changed? The horse standing still at the mounting block.
2. Is the behaviour being strengthened (occurring more often) or weakened (occurring less often)? Strengthened
3. What is the consequence to the horse's behaviour? Rider holds the reins tightly until the horse stands still and then releases them (although this is not recommended and only used as an example).
4. Was the consequence an addition to the horse's environment or a removal? A removal (the uncomfortable tightness of the reins is removed when the horse stands still).

The horse's behaviour is being adapted through **Negative Reinforcement**.

A single behaviour can potentially be affected by any of the four forms of consequence. When training, we must be aware of exactly which of the four potential consequences we are using to change our horse's behaviour. Without true understanding of why the horse is adapting his behaviour as he is, we cannot train effectively. Being able to identify and use these consequences to affect the horse's behaviour through operant conditioning is the first step to successful training. Each form of learning will be discussed in detail in the following chapters, further explaining the theory and practical application of the different forms of learning in training.

LEARNING RECAP

Reiterating the key points of this chapter and the most important concepts to understand to make your training as successful as possible.

Key Terms	Recap of Definition and Important Concepts
Positive reinforcement	Positive reinforcement is the adding of a pleasurable stimulus to the horse's learning environment as a consequence of a behaviour, encouraging a behaviour to occur more often in the future.
Negative reinforcement	Negative reinforcement is simply the removing of an unpleasant stimulus in consequence of a behaviour.
Positive punishment	Positive punishment is the addition of an adverse stimulus as a consequence of a behaviour. The addition of an unpleasant stimulus discourages the behaviour from occurring in the future because it is undesirable for the horse.
Negative punishment	Negative punishment is the removal of something good from the horse as a consequence of a behaviour.

Other Laws and Factors in Learning

THE FINAL LAW – EXTINCTION

The final law of learning is the Law of Extinction which states that if a previously reinforced behaviour ceases to be reinforced, the behaviour will decrease in frequency and eventually not occur at all. Hence the term 'extinction'.

In order for extinction of the behaviour to occur completely, the reinforcement of that behaviour must be absolutely terminated. Any reinforcement will continue to maintain the behaviour and extinction will not occur. Extinction is often not seen in mugging horses because the owner accidentally rewards them for the behaviour by giving the horse attention or a treat occasionally. Even if the reward is only very sporadic it will be enough that the horse is always hopeful that he may gain some reward for the behaviour and he may in fact become more persistent in his pursuit of the reward.

> **Note**: Extinction will only occur if there is no self-reinforcing aspect to the behaviour, or a strong reason for the behaviour occurring in the first place, such as a physical issue (pain) or a strong psychological issue (phobia). For example, some horses will chew their reins, but ignoring this behaviour will not cause extinction because the horse is often chewing the reins for a reason, i.e. anticipation, worry, toothache or habit. Extinction can sometimes work on horses that have learnt to head butt their owners for attention. Ignoring the horse during this behaviour could cause extinction of the behaviour.

A good study of how extinction can be effectively and, conversely, ineffectively applied is to observe toddlers at the supermarket. Most toddlers will eventually throw a tantrum when told they are not allowed an item they desire (usually sweets). The mother will respond in one of two ways:

- She bravely ignores the child's tantrums and the displeased looks of passers-by.
- After 10 minutes she gives in to the child's demands.

Child one will eventually learn that tantrums achieve nothing and will start to behave at the supermarket – extinction of the tantrum behaviour. However, child two, having been rewarded for his past attempts to pierce the eardrums of all nearby shoppers, will scream longer and harder next time in the hope of reward. If this time the mother gives in after 20 minutes of crying, the child learns that he needs to cry for 20 minutes in order to receive his reward. So instead of stopping the tantrum behaviour by leaving longer before rewarding, the mother is in fact teaching the child to throw larger and longer tantrums. Once the child has learned to cry for so long, extinction of the behaviour will also take much more persistence than if the behaviour had not been rewarded from the start. Extinction of a behaviour, achieved by the termination of all reward for that behaviour, is known as 'extinction by omission' (ignoring the unwanted behaviour: child one in the example).

However, extinction of a previously rewarded behaviour can also be induced by discontinuing the association between the reinforcement and the behaviour by rewarding other unassociated behaviours, or indeed randomly on some occasions. This method of extinction is harder to apply but can be just as effective if applied appropriately. For example, if the horse has learned to perform a trick, such as pawing or begging, for treats but the trick was never given a cue, the horse will perform the trick at any point when he thinks that a reward may be available. To extinguish this response to the presence of food completely, simply reward the horse at random times when the food is present. This will disassociate the behaviour and the reward in the horse's mind and as such, teach the horse that the behaviour is not beneficial and does not attract reward. After the behaviour has become fully disassociated from the reward, the behaviour will become extinguished and the horse will no longer perform the behaviour in the presence of food.

Note: When using extinction you will often find that the behaviour will get worse before it gets better. This is simply the horse attempting to get the response he is used to and it should be short-lived, as long as the response is not given.

Extinction can be made even more successful by integrating the technique with the reinforcement of other desirable behaviours. The horse should switch to performing these reinforced behaviours and not the ones that are being targeted for extinction. It is a behavioural rule that horses (and in fact, all animals) will prefer to carry out those behaviours that are most successful for them. Given a choice, horses will always choose to perform those behaviours that are most advantageous to them.

Extinction Bursts

When the horse is unlearning a previous behaviour you will get occurrences of extinction bursts. An extinction burst is a reoccurrence of the behaviour which is no longer rewarded or reinforced. These should be short-lived, as long as the behaviour is not being inadvertently reinforced. The best policy is to ignore these extinction bursts. If they are persistent, analyse whether they are being reinforced by your training or by the environment.

During all training, if the horse is unlearning a behaviour or a bad habit, you may find that for a while the horse will return to his old habits. This occurs because the new response/behaviour pattern is not yet fully established as the dominant response. Once the new response or non-response is established, the horse will not resort to these old habits and thus no extinction burst of the behaviour will occur.

For example, often you may find that once you have done the 'don't mug me' training, to train or retrain a horse not to snatch treats, very occasionally the horse may try to look in your pocket for the next few weeks. As long as the horse never receives the reward and the trainer insists on the 'look away', the snatching behaviour will disappear completely.

Why Do Extinction Bursts Occur?

When a horse is learning a new behaviour or task, or unlearning a previously reinforced task such as not to mug, the new behaviour is competing with the old behaviour to become the dominant response to use in that situation. Reinforcing the new behaviour (for example, the looking away in the no mugging training) will, after a period of time, make it more established and more likely to occur than the old behaviour (mugging). The more often and more strongly the new behaviour is reinforced, the faster it is likely to become the dominant response. However, until this becomes fully established as the dominant behaviour, the old pattern may make an occasional appearance. As long as it is not encouraged by being reinforced, the old behaviour should occur less and less until it disappears, and the new behaviour becomes the dominant behaviour.

UNDERSTANDING GENERALISATION AND DISCRIMINATION LEARNING IN TRAINING

During training it is often necessary for the horse to transfer learned cues, behaviours or responses to other situations or other objects in his environment. Alternatively, it is also sometimes necessary for the horse to learn to discriminate between objects or situations during training. These two processes are known as generalisation and discrimination respectively.

Generalisation

When training young foals, they are often first taught to lead from the halter whilst walking behind their dam (mother). This learned leading behaviour is then transferred to leading away from the dam and then in different situations, such as in the schooling area, through fields, at show grounds and even possibly while out hacking, being lead by a handler who is mounted on another horse. This process of the young horse learning to transfer the learned leading behaviour to different situations and environments is known as generalisation.

Generalisation is simply achieved by encouraging the desired learned behaviour to occur in the new environment by creating a situation in which the horse can achieve the response, i.e. asking for a behaviour which is well established and easy for the horse to achieve and then rewarding the production of the desired behaviour in a different environment. The training can then be built up to incorporate harder behaviours and more complicated responses as the horse gets accustomed to working in the new situation.

Horses can also generalise their response to cue stimuli. For example, if the horse is taught to move away from a gentle pressure in one direction he can often quickly generalise this response to the pressure cue and move away from the pressure in other directions. The same process is used when encouraging the horse to generalise a response to different objects; establish the behaviour with the original object and then ask the horse to perform the required response to the new object, rewarding the horse when he performs the correct response. Again, make it as simple as possible for the horse to achieve the correct response. Never punish the horse for offering the wrong response; at least he is trying to understand what you require from him. Simply don't reward incorrect behaviours or responses and continue to encourage the horse to produce the correct behaviour or an approximation of it.

This process is a vital part of good horse training. If the horse is only ever asked for a certain response or behaviour in one environment, it is unlikely that he will replicate that response easily when placed in a different environment. For example, if the horse is only ever trained for dressage in the school or arena, he may struggle to transfer the moves to a grass surface or to the show ground. Once a movement has been taught to your horse for dressage, show jumping or the show ring in the arena, ensure that the movement is then transferred to different environment and surfaces. When asking for the behaviour or response in a new environment or situation, it may be necessary to ask for a easier version of the behaviour and work back up to the original level achieved. Taking a step back in training can facilitate the horse's production of the taught behaviour in new environments without needing to place additional pressure on the horse, especially if the environment to which you wish the response to be generalised is more exciting or distracting than the original one. When first training for any competition discipline, competing in a class lower than the level at which you work at home can help the horse to generalise his learned responses to the show ground, until he is used to working at show grounds.

Generalisation is not just a skill for competition horses and trainers, it is also vital for anyone wishing to enjoy contented hacking out with their horse. For example, when the horse first learns to open gates or to stand for mounting, he is likely to have learned these skills in the yard or schooling arena. However, these skills are also essential when out hacking and need to be generalised to situations away from the yard or school arena so that the horse can easily perform the desired behaviours when out hacking.

Horses can also learn to generalise responses between objects. When the horse is first introduced to the bit he will be taught to open his mouth for the bit to be placed behind the front teeth. The horse will over time be required to generalise this response and open his mouth for different types of bits, from snaffles to straight bar bits and even double bridles. Similarly when teaching a horse to jump, the horse will also need to generalise the response from poles to cavalletti and then to crosspoles, straight bars and spread. Later it will also be necessary for the horse to generalise the jump response to objects such as fillers and cross-country fences. Again, when introducing the horse to new types of jump it may be necessary to go back to a lower height in order to ensure that the horse can easily succeed in the new situation and build confidence and ability without becoming worried or overfaced.

Also be aware that generalisation can occur when not desired. For example, most horses will generalise any squeezing of the lower leg to be a 'pick up your foot' command rather than only lifting the leg to a more specific cue. This makes checking the legs for injury more difficult as the horse will think that the handler wishes him to lift his legs. If an undesired generalisation occurs during training it can be corrected by teaching the horse to discriminate between responses, situations or objects.

Discrimination

It is sometimes also necessary to teach your horse to discriminate between different situations and objects with regard to how he behaves in that environment or in response to the object. For example, stallions must learn from a young age when courtship behaviours are required and not required. The stallion should be taught not to show courtship behaviours when being handled or ridden and only when in breeding situations. Some studs have a certain type of bridle the horse wears only when he is being used for breeding so the horse learns to discriminate between the bridle objects and their meanings. Discrimination learning is also needed when the horse is learning to be ridden with other horses. The horse must learn to discriminate between appropriate social behaviour when loose with other horses, and when being ridden and handled around other horses.

Discrimination can be encouraged by only rewarding behaviours or responses when they occur in the situation desired or with regard to the object desired, and not in any others. It may also be necessary to prevent the horse from performing the behaviour in other situations. This can be done using a variety of techniques; see Chapter 10 on dealing with unwanted behaviours without using punishment for more information on this. For example, if you required the horse to discriminate between two different targets, say a large cone and a small cone (only ever targeting the large cone), you would only ever reward the horse for touching the large cone and ignore his attempts to target the small cone. The horse will soon realise it is only beneficial to touch the large cone and to discriminate between the two. This process can be quickly replicated with any objects or situations you wish the horse to be able to discriminate between, by simply rewarding the horse only for responding to the object or in the situation you wish the horse to respond to.

Similarly, the horse can learn to discriminate between situations and objects in training when not necessary. If this occurs, simply encourage the horse to generalise their response by rewarding him for displaying the correct response in more situations and to more objects. For example, when most people first teach a horse to leg yield, they practise the movement from the three-quarter line of the school to the track. If the horse is only asked for the movement in this manner, he may discriminate the response, only understanding the request for the movement in this situation. Therefore, to ensure the horse understands the leg yield aid and to generalise the response to all situations where the response is asked for, the leg yield should also be taught and rewarded toward and away from the track direction, on circles, spirals and on hacks.

Can Horses Discriminate and Generalise Between Stimuli?

Smith and Goldman (1998) investigated whether horses could discriminate between grey and one of four other colours (red, green, yellow and blue). Four Arabian horses and one thoroughbred were used in the study. The criterion for having learned to discriminate between the colours was set at 85% correct responses, and the experimental test was for colour versus grey discriminations. Greys of different intensities were used so that brightness was an irrelevant cue. Three of the horses were tested with all the colours. Two of the horses learned to discriminate between all four colours and different intensities of grey. The third horse learned to discriminate with red and blue, but not with yellow and green. The fourth and fifth horses were only tested with green and yellow and with blue respectively, and both performed the discriminations above the learning criterion of 85% correct responses. It was concluded that horses have at least dichromatic colour vision, but that some individuals may have less ability to discriminate on the basis of colour due to vision differences. This study also tells us that horses can learn to discriminate between many similar stimuli during training and that in training individual differences in horses must be considered.

Discrimination learning in horses has also allowed the investigation of other forms of learning. For example, Sappington and Goldman (1994) found that some horses could discriminate on the basis of a shape pattern concept, such as triangularity. Furthermore, Hanggi (2003) found that horses in the study could discriminate on the basis of a relative size concept (whether an object is bigger or smaller than another) but also that they could generalise the concept of discrimination learning to different types of stimuli. For example, the horse could pick out the larger or smaller of the objects regardless of shape, texture, colour or two-dimensional versus three-dimensional objects. These studies show us that horses are capable of different forms of learning, including some concept learning, and also that they can be very proficient at discrimination and generalisation training tasks.

LEARNING RECAP

Reiterating the key points of this chapter and the most important concepts to understand to make your training as successful as possible.

Key Terms	Recap of Definition and Important Concepts
Extinction	If a previously reinforced behaviour ceases to be reinforced the behaviour will decrease in frequency and eventually not occur at all.
Extinction bursts	An extinction burst is a reoccurrence of the behaviour which is no longer rewarded or reinforced. It should be short-lived as long as the behaviour is not being inadvertently reinforced.
Generalisation	Generalisation is the transferring of a learned response to different and novel situations or objects in the horse's environment.
Discrimination	Discrimination refers to the ability of the horse to distinguish between different and novel situations and objects in his environment and respond appropriately.

The Power of Positive Reinforcement

Positive reinforcement is one of the most powerful tools in our possession for motivating the horse to enjoy his training and actively participate in the learning process. Although the horse can be motivated to work through punishment and negative reinforcement, he will be doing so out of a wish to avoid undesirable situations, rather than because he truly desires to work with the trainer.

To recap: positive reinforcement is the adding of a pleasurable stimulus to the horse's learning environment as a consequence of a behaviour, encouraging that behaviour to occur more often in the future.

Both intrinsic and extrinsic forms of positive reinforcement exist. **Intrinsic positive reinforcement** is an inherent part of the behavior that is being reinforced. An example of intrinsic reinforcement would be social grooming behaviour, as social grooming is naturally rewarding for the horse. **Extrinsic positive reinforcement** is reinforcement that occurs following a behavior, but is not inherently a part of that behaviour. An example of this would be giving the horse a food treat for backing up nicely or performing a schooling move particularly well. Backing up or doing the schooling move is not inherently rewarding to the horse; the reward is added as the consequence by the trainer.

WHAT CAN BE A POSITIVE REINFORCER?

Positive reinforcement can be primary or secondary. **Primary reinforcers** are stimuli that are considered naturally rewarding, i.e. food, being scratched or stroked (but only if the horse enjoys these stimuli). Horses will find these stimuli more or less rewarding, depending on their individual personalities. For example, horses that don't like to be touched will not find being stroked or scratched a particularly rewarding experience. Similarly, horses who are not overly concerned about food rewards will not find being rewarded with titbits as reinforcing as a horse who is food obsessed.

Secondary reinforcers are stimuli that have become associated with rewarding stimuli and thus have been conditioned to be rewarding for the horse. The 'click' used during clicker training is conditioned to be rewarding because of the association between the click and a food reward. Another example of a secondary reinforcer is verbal praise. The praise itself has no intrinsic value to the horse but when combined with scratches or treats, the praise can develop an association with reward. Primary reinforcers are normally much more rewarding to the horse than secondary reinforcers.

When working with your horse it is necessary to know which reinforcers he finds most rewarding. Every horse is different and in order to get the most from each horse it is important to know which reinforcer is most rewarding to him, be it food rewards or scratches, and how he responds to secondary reinforcers. Knowing these things about a horse will allow you to make training as enjoyable as possible, while also motivating the horse to participate willingly.

WHICH REINFORCER SHOULD I USE?

Food Reinforcers

Food is possibly the strongest reinforcer for the majority of horses. The strength of various food reinforcers obviously varies with the preferences of each individual horse. Usually sweeter food treats, such as apples, carrots and mints, are stronger reinforcers. When using food reinforcers it is often a good idea to have more than one type of treat as this will optimise the horse's motivation. However, if the horse is overly enthusiastic about food rewards, the opposite, i.e. only using one form of food reinforcer, can often be beneficial, by reducing the horse's enthusiasm.

One strong advantage of using food rewards is that they are easy to apply to training. They can be given easily and quickly to the horse without disrupting training.

There are many myths which surround the use of food rewards, most of which are false.

Myth 1: Using Food Rewards Will Cause My Horse to Bite Me and/or Mug Me.

Using food rewards does not induce biting in the horse. Feeding the horse the rewards for the mugging behaviour will encourage nipping and biting, but this can be prevented or trained out by doing the 'don't mug me' training task (described in Chapter 3). Food treats can be used with most horses, as long as the 'don't mug me' rule is firmly understood.

Myth 2: If I Use Food Rewards, the Horse Will Only Perform When I Have Food on Me

Food is used as a reward for the behaviour, not to induce the performance of the behaviour once it has been learned. Therefore the horse will perform the behaviour regardless of the presence of food. Using an appropriate schedule of reinforcement (to be discussed later) will also ensure that the use of food serves only to increase the performance of the horse and the relationship between horse and handler.

Myth 3: Using Food Is Equivalent to Bribery

The concept of bribery implies that the horse is corrupting his moral behaviour by accepting the food. The horse has no morals and, as such, is incapable of being corrupted. A better analogy for the use of food in training would be giving the horse a wage for his hard work. The wage motivates the horse and encourages him to actively work with the handler, rather than to perform out of fear of consequences, as is often the case if only negative reinforcement and punishment are used. Using a positive reinforcement such as food can also encourage problem-solving abilities and an enthusiasm for work in the horse, which would not be created if the food were merely a bribe.

The Use of Different Food Rewards in Training

It is important to note that different food rewards can have very different motivational properties and hence be an important factor to consider in training. Ninomiya *et al.* (2007) investigated the use and effect of different rewards during training and subsequently changing the rewards. Two forms of food reward were used in the study – hay and a more palatable pellet food. First, the authors tested whether there was any difference in terms of the horse learning new operant responses (behaviour). No difference was found in the time it took for the horses to acquire the new behaviour response despite the difference in reward palatability. However, the study did find that if the food reward was changed from the more palatable pellet to the hay, the number of rewards achieved significantly decreased and in fact, the change of reward caused extinction of the newly acquired responses in three of the tested horses, meaning that the horse would no longer perform the new behaviours for the reward. It was also found that if the reward was changed during training from the hay to the pellet, the horse would achieve significantly more rewards. The investigators concluded that the palatability of reward is not necessarily too important for the training of the horse (as long as it has some desirability). However, it is necessary to consider carefully which reward to use if the reward type needs to be changed, in order to maintain response rate and allow the ability to change back to the old reward if necessary. Changing to a more palatable reward and back to a lesser one may also lower response rate. Maintaining reward palatability is thus important for consistency in training.

When Not to Use Food

Food can be used as a suitable and effective reward with most horses. However, horses that may have issues with the use of food as a reward include those who have been starved or those who have become protective over their food. These horses can often still be trained using food as a reward, but they may show behaviours such as aggression to begin with. In such instances, it is often best to seek professional advice.

A good first step would be to do the 'don't mug me' training (see Chapter 3). If the horse displays extreme aggression or anxiety, the best policy is to ignore the reaction whilst keeping the situation, yourself and the horse safe (over a stable door if necessary). Carry on training the horse within the 'don't mug me' structure; only reward the horse when he is standing calmly and away from the handler. The horse should quickly learn to behave calmly around food. If he does not start to behave calmly relatively quickly, it may be necessary to seek help or to not use food within your training.

Food may also not be a suitable reward for horses that are uninterested in food. Although most horses can be motivated by their favourite appetiser, there are some who are not motivated by any form of food reward. These horses are best trained using another form of reward.

Jackpotting

If the horse gives a response which is a particularly good example of the desired behaviour, giving a larger or more exciting reward can increase the chances of getting a good response the next time. Make sure that 'jackpots' don't occur too often or they will lose their effect; save them for the really good efforts.

Stroking, Scratching, Petting or Patting

Horses who are fond of being petted will consider it a reward and it can be used as such within training. Most horses have a couple of spots on their body which they enjoy having rubbed or scratched. It is very useful for both the training of the horse and your relationship with him to find these spots. It has been said that patting is not a reward for a horse. I personally have found that a gentle pat can be as rewarding for some horses as a stroke. Most horses, however, seem to most enjoy a good scratch (Fig. 6.1).

It is possible for the horse to be rewarded with petting in the same way as with a food reward, although it is often harder to apply during training. For example, if the horse has done a particularly nice jump or two but likes to be scratched underneath his belly, the rider

Figure 6.1   Some horses enjoy petting enough for it to be used as positive reinforcement.

would have to leap off and stand there scratching the horse in the middle of the jumping session!

Petting does, however, teach the horse that human touch can be pleasurable, particularly useful in mistrustful or nervous animals. The human–horse bond can be greatly increased by getting the horse to be comfortable when being touched all over his body and even to enjoy it.

WHEN TO REWARD

Knowing when to reward is crucial to the success of training, and for keeping the horse's attention and maintaining a steady work rate from the horse. When any behaviour is first being taught it is imperative that every response is rewarded. This ensures that the horse is absolutely confident that he is performing the correct behaviour. Rewarding every response is known as a continuous reinforcement. Once the correct response is received from the horse every time the behaviour is asked for, then he can be put on a schedule of reinforcement.

There are several schedules of reinforcement that can be employed when training using positive reinforcement. A schedule of reinforcement defines when the horse is rewarded for the behaviour. The schedule keeps the horse work rate consistent, while not requiring that every response is rewarded. In fact, not rewarding every response keeps the horse more interested in the work. This may seem illogical but a good analogy of this effect would be that rewarding every response is similar to using a vending machine; if you do the behaviour of putting in the money, you expect the reward of the chocolate bar. However, using a schedule of reinforcement is similar to playing a slot machine; despite the lack of reward for every behaviour of putting the money into the game, the promise of a reward maintains the behaviour. B.F. Skinner (mentioned in Chapter 4) is said to have discovered that animals can maintain the same rate of response, despite the reduced reward, when his lab ran low on reward pellets and thus discovered the schedules of reinforcement.

There are four possible schedules of reinforcement:

*   fixed ratio
*   variable ratio
*   fixed duration
*   variable duration.

	Ratio	Duration
Fixed	Fixed Ratio	Fixed Duration
Variable	Variable Ratio	Variable Duration

Fixed Schedules of Reinforcement

Fixed Ratio Schedule of Reinforcement

During a fixed ratio schedule of reinforcement the horse is rewarded for a certain number of responses given. For example, a reward may be given for every fourth correct rein back or every sixth time the horse lifts his leg nicely. The number is decided by the trainer and doesn't vary; it always requires the same number of operant responses from the horse to produce the reward from the trainer. Employees who are set targets of production or sales for extra wages are on a fixed ratio schedule of reinforcement because it requires a set amount of a behaviour to achieve the reward.

Fixed Duration Schedule of Reinforcement

Fixed duration reinforcement schedules are used when it is most efficient to reward the horse after a fixed amount of time of correct response behaviour. For example, if teaching a horse to 'stay', one could reward him after every one minute of the desired behaviour.

Advantages of Fixed Schedules of Reinforcement

Fixed ratio schedules can be advantageous because it is easy for the trainer to remember when to reward the horse. The fixed ratio can also be used to create an accelerated number of responses, or continued response before the reward, as the horse will be able to predict when the reward is due. When humans play a computer game they know how much play is necessary until the next reward of going up a level; because of this, the game-playing behaviour will often increase as the end of level approaches.

If a horse is required to perform a behaviour for a determined amount of time or number of responses, each time the behaviour is asked for, a fixed schedule of reinforcement can be useful to ensure that the required number of responses or length of response is achieved.

Disadvantages of Fixed Schedules of Reinforcement

Horses are very efficient learners and will often realise that the reward is only given after a certain number of responses or a set amount of time. Due to this prediction of the coming reward, the horse will not only accelerate his response up until the reward, but may also hesitate to perform the behaviour again after the reward has been given. Similar to horses, humans experience this dip in performance after reaching a reward. Computer gamers will pause after reaching a new level and target-driven workers will drop their work rate after reaching a target, before accelerating their rate as the reward once again gets closer. Fixed schedules of reinforcement are best used when this dip in work rate can be incorporated easily.

Variable Schedules of Reinforcement

Variable Ratio Schedules of Reinforcement

A variable ratio schedule of reinforcement is the reinforcement of behaviour after an unpredictable number of correct responses. For example, the horse may be rewarded for the third correct transition during schooling, then for the sixth and the second, etc. Make sure that the number of responses is as unpredictable as possible; often it is easy to start slipping into rewarding every few responses, so that the horse can begin to predict when the reward is due.

Variable Duration Schedules of Reinforcement

Variable duration schedules of reinforcement consist of rewarding the horse after varying amounts of time of a correct behaviour response, i.e. after 30 seconds from the initial command, then after one minute from first response to the command. For example, a nervous horse could be rewarded for acting calmly at variable durations to encourage the calm behaviour or, when teaching a horse to salute (jambette), the leg lift can be rewarded after varying durations of the correct response.

Advantages of Variable Schedules of Reinforcement

A variable schedule of reinforcement ensures that the horse is kept guessing as to when the reward is due, and thus is kept enthusiastic for the next reward. It is this promise of reward, without the ability to predict its timing, which keeps people playing gambling machines. Due to the unpredictable timing of the reward, the performance of the horse's behavioural response is kept more consistent, as the post-reward dip in performance in eliminated.

The variable schedule of reinforcement also ensures that, should the reinforcer become limited or stop, e.g. you have forgotten your titbits for a training session, the horse will often keep responding longer than horses on fixed reinforcement schedules. Horses that have to stay on tasks for a long time, for example riding school horses, where the time between the first command, i.e. at the beginning of a lunge lesson, and the end of the task, i.e. the end of the lunge lesson, may be of a considerable duration, may benefit from and be more motivated by a variable interval schedule of reinforcement.

Disadvantages of Variable Schedules of Reinforcement

Variable ratio schedules are more difficult to use and, if the trainer is inexperienced, they may tend to not reward often enough while trying to randomise the schedule, which may inhibit the horse's performance. Alternatively, the trainer may start rewarding every few responses so that the schedule becomes predictable and fixed in nature, and so the horse starts to predict and expect the reward. The schedule must be truly randomised for best results.

Work Rates Achieved on Different Schedules of Reinforcement

The different schedules of reinforcement create different work rates in the horse. Fixed schedules of reinforcement create accelerations and dips in the work rate whereas variable schedules of reinforcement develop a smooth work rate. The dips in the fixed ratio have occurred because the horse knows how much work is required for the next reward and as such is likely to pause after the reward is received. The horse on the variable schedule cannot predict when the next reward is due and so will maintain the same rate of work throughout training, as the next reward could appear after the next response or time period (Fig. 6.2).

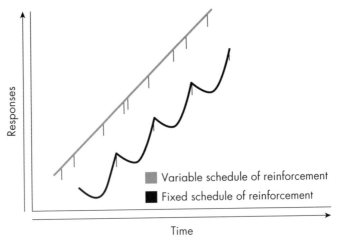

Variable schedule of reinforcement
Fixed schedule of reinforcement

Time

Responses

Figure 6.2   Graphical representation of the performance created by the use of fixed and variable schedules of reinforcement.

Why do Variable Schedules Work in Positive Reinforcement?

The area of the brain which controls an animal's experience of reward is called the basal ganglia and it is controlled by the activity of a chemical called dopamine. During the early phase of training, when the reward for a behaviour is new to the horse, this part of the brain activates when the reward is received (Schultz 1998). This activation creates pleasant feelings for the horse and encourages him to repeat the behaviour in order to receive another reward. However, once the horse is certain of the behaviour or cue which predicts the arrival of the reward, and can reproduce the behaviour and receive the reward easily, the reward part of the brain starts to activate on the performance of the behaviour or on the cue (Schultz 1998). It is the behaviour or cue which is now rewarding to the horse. This is why a greater motivation to be involved in the training process is often seen in horses and other animals trained using reward, because the work itself becomes rewarding to them. This reward for work does not occur with other forms of training such as negative reinforcement and punishment. It is this rewarding activation of the dopamine neurons for predicting cues and behaviours which keeps the horse's motivation high on the variable schedule of reward because the horse still receives a rewarding experience from the training even when not every correct response is being rewarded.

It could also be considered that in terms of evolution, it is more beneficial for variable reinforcement to maintain rather than inhibit work rates in the horse. There are few responses in the horse's natural environment that will receive reward every time the response is executed. For example, if you are a horse who has learned to paw through snow to uncover food it is unlikely that every paw through the snow will uncover food, so therefore not every behaviour response is resulting in reward. Similarly if you are a stallion trying to approach a mare, your advances will not always be rewarded with courtship and in some cases may indeed be punished with a swift kick. However, if the horse was to stop looking for food or seeking a mate because sometimes the response did not receive the desired reward, he would be less likely to survive and breed than one whose motivation and work rate stayed high despite some unrewarded responses. This is because the horse who continues searching for mates and food, even if he is sometimes unsuccessful, is more likely to receive more rewards (food and courtship) overall than horses that stop the reward-predicting behaviour when not rewarded for the behaviour. Therefore horses, like other species, can work happily on a variable schedule. Obviously if the response is never rewarded, i.e. food is never found under the snow, the response will eventually be extinguished.

Is it Disappointing for the Horse to be Put on a Variable Schedule of Reinforcement?

I am often asked if horses resent or are disappointed by being put on a variable schedule of reinforcement. The simple answer is no. As long as the horse is still being rewarded at a suitable rate you should see no resentment or disappointment from your horse in response to being put on a variable schedule of reinforcement. If the variable reinforcement schedule is not suitable and the horses is not rewarded often enough within the schedule, a decrease in work rate will be seen. For example, if the horse has gone from being rewarded every time on a continuous schedule during initial training to being rewarded variably but is being asked to perform upwards of 20 responses for the reward, of course his work rate will decrease. The variable schedule needs to be more randomised and if necessary gradually increased if it is necessary for the horse to perform so many responses before reward. Being observant of work rate and moving quickly from the continuous to the variable reinforcement schedule once a behaviour is learned will prevent the horse's work rate dropping or any emotional side effects occurring during training.

TRAINING USING POSITIVE REINFORCEMENT

Training using positive reinforcement should be applied as shown in Fig. 6.3.

Identifying Targets

Before you start teaching a new task to your horse make sure you have identified exactly what your goal behaviour is. This will help structure your training and ensure that confusion doesn't inhibit the training. It can even be helpful to write your goals down.

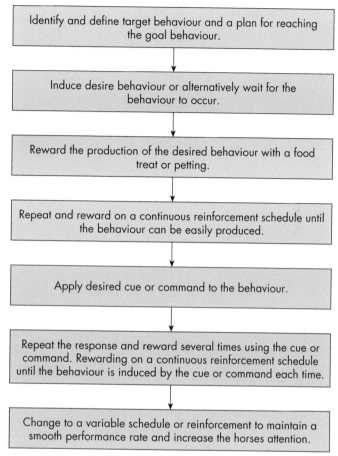

Figure 6.3 Training using positive reinforcement.

Inducing the Desired Behaviour

The desired behaviour can be induced or shaped (which will be discussed in Chapter 11). If the behaviour is likely to occur naturally, wait until it occurs of its own accord, then reward immediately. This will ensure that the behaviour is more likely to occur in the future.

Never induce a behaviour using any method which would cause the horse to be fearful or in discomfort, otherwise the value of the reward for the produced behaviour will be dramatically decreased and the likelihood of the desired behaviour reoccurring will also be reduced.

Luring

Luring is a technique used in dog training which I have found to be useful in some horse training sessions, to reduce the amount of pressure used with the horse. Luring occurs when the desired behaviour is induced by giving the horse something really desirable to focus on and to follow, such as food. Once trained, a target can also be used to induce a behaviour, without the need for pressure. The lure is only used to induce the behaviour at the beginning of training. Once the command or cue is added, it will take over from the lure and the lure is removed.

Teaching Targeting for Luring

Targeting can be taught using positive reinforcement operant conditioning, but it is often easier to teach targeting using clicker training, as explained in the next chapter.

First, have a piece of equipment to hand that the horse can use as a target. This can either be a professional target stick, a fly swat, a

Figure 6.4   Louie demonstrating targeting.

plastic bottle tied firmly to a stick or anything else which is safe and large enough for the horse to easily touch with his nose.

Hold the target in front of the horse. Most horses are curious and will touch the target with their nose to investigate (Fig. 6.4). When the horse touches the target give him the reward (food is the easiest, and usually most effective, reward to use) and praise immediately. Repeat this routine many times until the horse touches the target reliably wherever it is placed. A command or cue can then be added to the target behaviour, for example you could say 'target'. Once the horse touches the target reliably on command switch him to a variable schedule of reinforcement.

If the horse is worried about the target, reward any movement towards the target and any investigation of the target. When the horse touches the target with his nose give him extra praise and a large reward and then continue as above. Once the horse has learned to touch the target it can be used to induce desired behaviours without the need for force.

Cues and Commands

Tips for Introducing Commands

As humans, we tend to overuse language. When teaching a new task to the horse, make sure that the command is not introduced until the behaviour can be reliably induced in the horse. Saying a command while the behaviour is not being performed only causes the horse to associate the command with the wrong behaviour. Many owners forget that their horse cannot understand human words. For example, how many times have you heard owners incessantly repeating the word 'stand' to a fidgeting horse, assuming the horse has some amazing ability to infer the meaning of this strange sound.

The command should only be given once the desired behaviour is being performed and then it should be immediately rewarded. This way the correct behaviour is associated with the command. After a few repetitions of saying the command during the behaviour, the command will become meaningful to the horse. Once the meaning of the command has been established the horse will perform the behaviour on the command. To test whether your horse has established the meaning of the command, simply say the command. If he does not perform the desired behaviour, he does not yet understand the meaning of the command.

Tips for Effective Commands

Always say commands in a higher pitched (although not squeaky) and friendly voice. This type of voice is more appealing to the horse and will separate commands from the rest of your speech, helping the command to be established faster. Never use a stern voice as this can sound like scolding and is unnecessary. It will also not encourage your horse to work for you.

Choose words which you haven't overused around your horse; for example, use 'stay' which is less common than 'stand' when training your horse to stand still. Only say the command once, so that it is precise and distinct. Repeating the command will not make it clearer to the horse, and may result him expecting to be told more than once before he performs the behaviour.

Signals can be taught just as easily as voice commands.

Try to make the commands for each behaviour as different from each other as possible, so that the training is very clear.

Tips for Introducing Cues

Applying cues is very similar to applying commands. A cue can be any movement of the body you wish to use to communicate to the horse; for example, holding a hand in the air to signal to the horse to stay still, or beckoning to the horse to call him over. Once again, the cue should only be added to signal the start of the behaviour once the behaviour can be reliably induced; this ensures that the cue is only given for the desirable behaviour. Again, once the meaning of the cue has been established the horse will perform the behaviour on the cue. The test of whether your horse has established the meaning of the cue is also the same; simply give the cue and if the horse does not perform the desired behaviour, he does not yet understand the meaning of the cue.

Tips for Effective Cues

Make sure the cue is clear to the horse. Although the cue itself doesn't have to be large, it has to be distinguishable by the horse.

Make sure the cue is a movement that the horse does not see from you unless you want that certain behaviour. If the cue is ambiguous the response will not be as good as it would be with a clear cue. Again, try to only give the cue clearly, once.

Make sure the cue is visible to the horse. This sounds obvious, but it is surprising how inaccurate peripheral vision is in both humans and horses, so avoid giving cues in this area if possible or make them very distinct. Also remember the horse's blind spots (Fig. 6.5).

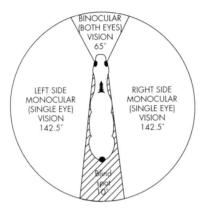

Figure 6.5 Equine field of vision.

The Importance of Timing

Good timing is a skill crucial to successful training using positive reinforcement methods. The association between the desired behaviour and the reward is of the utmost importance, as it is this association which ensures the likelihood of the desired behaviour being performed in the future. Bad timing can cause the wrong behaviour to be rewarded and thus reinforced, or even cause the horse to become confused as to which behaviour the trainer desires.

At the beginning of training it is necessary for the reward to be consistent and immediate until the desired behaviour is fully understood by the horse. The closer the reward is in time and space to the desired behaviour, the stronger the association between the behaviour and the reward. It is this close association which will create the understanding between horse and handler as to which behaviour is desired for the reward. Once this understanding is established, the horse can be changed to the variable schedule of reinforcement, as understanding is no longer the goal but rather continued motivation and a desire to learn and try.

Timing is a skill in horse training that is learnt not only through the study of literature, but also from practice in training horses using positive reinforcement and learning from mistakes.

The timing of sessions and tasks is also important. Don't make any session too long. The horse should end the session still eager to work and participate. The length of the session will depend on the horse's age and fitness. Don't expect young or immature horses to be able to concentrate for long periods and, similarly, old horses may struggle if the session is too long. If the horse is physically unfit, shorter sessions are beneficial, especially if the work is physically demanding. Regular breaks are also beneficial during schooling, to refresh the horse mentally and physically. During these breaks allow the horse to run and play, or to rest, as is most appropriate.

Reward the Try

Rewarding the try, or shaping, will be discussed in more depth in Chapter 11. For now I will just say that, as a trainer, you should make sure that you don't ask the horse to make too large a step during the training; make sure that every task you teach is broken down into easily managed steps. The goal behaviour is shaped, and eventually reached, by rewarding each step that is a near approximation to the goal behaviour. Breaking tasks down in this fashion ensures not only success for the horse but a quicker arrival at the goal behaviour, as the task is more likely to be understood. Furthermore, this easier success for the horse will encourage him to be confident, attentive and contented in his work.

The Use of Positive Reinforcement During Rehabilitation

Innes and McBride (2007) found that when positive and negative reinforcement methods were compared in their effectiveness during the rehabilitation of horses (to lead in hand, stand to be groomed, traverse an obstacle course and load into a trailer), there were significant differences between the two groups. Horses trained using positive reinforcement were more motivated to take part in the rehabilitation training and to display trial and error, or investigative behaviour, in new environments or training situations. Innes and McBride concluded that positive reinforcement could be beneficial to the training and welfare of horses going through a rehabilitation process.

Finally

These are the basics of applying positive reinforcement training using operant conditioning. It is unfortunate that positive reinforcement is often overlooked in the horse world as a method of training, because it can be a fantastically efficient and fun way to teach horses the skills they will require to lead a contented life with their human owners and trainers. Positive reinforcement can be used to teach any desired behaviour to the horse and is by no means limited to the examples explained in this chapter. Positive reinforcement will encourage a co-operative relationship between the horse and owner, where the horse actively seeks to be involved in the training process and is not there by restraint and the fear of consequences. Using positive reinforcement also makes training a very pleasant process for the horse, helping us to further forge a relationship with him. A relationship built through encouraging the horse to use his wits in collaboration with you, the trainer, rather than through harsh restraint and consequences, will be more joyful for both the horse and trainer and, as such, far more productive. The horse should see the time spent with the trainer as one of the best events of the day and even look forward to it.

LEARNING RECAP

Reiterating the key points of the chapter and the most important concepts to understand to make your training as successful as possible.

Key Terms	Recap of Definition and Important Concepts
Primary positive reinforcers	These are stimuli that are considered naturally rewarding, e.g. food.
Secondary reinforcers	These are stimuli that have become associated with rewarding stimuli and thus have been conditioned to be rewarding for the horse.
Jackpotting	If the horse gives a response which is a particularly good example of the desired behaviour, giving a larger or more exciting reward can increase the chances of getting a good response the next time.

Schedules of reinforcement	A schedule of reinforcement defines when the horse is rewarded for the behaviour. The schedule keeps the horse's work rate consistent, whilst not requiring that every response is rewarded. Schedules of reinforcement can be fixed (predictable) or variable (unpredictable) and can be based on the number of responses (ratio) or period of time displaying the correct behaviour (duration).
Rewarding the try	Make sure that every task you teach is broken down into easily managed steps. Each step should be a closer approximation of the final desired behaviour.
Setting targets	Always make sure you have a set target in mind for your training, so that the training is specific and efficient.
Inducing desired behaviours	Understand how to use luring and targeting to induce desired behaviours.

Training Task: Using Positive Reinforcement to Teach the Back, the Heel, the Stay, the Recall and the Yield

Teaching certain commands is essential for the safety of both handler and horse during training and in everyday life. It is very important that you can move your horse around effectively and control his movement, such as backing up, yielding over, standing still and staying with you. All of these commands can be taught with positive reinforcement using the techniques explained earlier in this chapter. Teaching these commands is explained step by step below.

The Back

First hold the treat in your fist. Place the fist at the horse's chest so that the horse has to move backwards to get the treat. As soon as he moves back a pace, open your hand and give the horse the reward and praise. Gradually increase the number of backwards paces needed to get the reward.

Once the horse understands the 'back' lure and responds reliably to it, a command or cue, such as 'back', can be added. Repeat the lure using the command or cue until the horse understands the signal, and then begin to remove the lure until the backing behaviour can be produced by the command or cue alone. When the behaviour is reliably produced at the presentation of the command or cue, the horse can be transferred from the continuous schedule of reinforcement (rewarding every response) to a variable schedule of reinforcement (reward the behaviour on a random basis) (Fig. 6.6).

The Heel

To teach the horse to follow you on command, simply encourage him to come with you using a food lure (Fig. 6.7). Reward the horse with the food occasionally for coming with you. Once the horse comes with you reliably, add a cue to the behaviour and reward using a variable schedule of reinforcement. The lure can be gradually removed once the cue for the behaviour reliably produces the heeling behaviour.

The Stay

Choose a time to teach the stay when your horse is calm; this will increase the likelihood of the horse standing still and succeeding in learning the stay. Once the stay is established, the horse should be expected to stay even if excited. First, set the horse up so that he is standing in a good position and in a calm manner. Then put your hand up, with the palm to the horse's face; this signals the stay. Walk a step back from your hand; the hand acts as a barrier to forward movement. If the horse stands reward him; if he moves, simply don't reward him and place him back in position (Fig. 6.8a).

Once the horse has been reward for this task a few times, gradually move further and further back and increase the length of the stay (Fig. 6.8b). If the horse gets confused at any point and starts moving during the stay, go back to an easier and shorter stay and increase the length once the horse has succeeded at the shorter stay. Once he will stay reliably to the hand signal, a voice command such as 'stay' or 'stand' can be added if desired.

(a)

(b)

Figure 6.6a,b   Dolly demonstrating the 'back' taught through luring.

Figure 6.7   Cola demonstrating the heel over a fence.

Figure 6.8a   Saffy demonstrating the stay.

Figure 6.8b   Saffy demonstrating a more advanced stay.

The Recall

Stand a little way from the horse and then show him the reward. When he comes to you for the reward, give him both the reward

Figure 6.9   Soli demonstrating the recall using the luring training technique.

and praise. Repeat this procedure until the horse comes to you reliably and over longer distances.

Again, once the horse understands the 'recall' lure and responds reliably to it, a command or cue, such as 'come', can be added. Repeat the lure, using the command or cue, until the horse understands the signal, and then begin to remove the lure until the recall behaviour can be induced by the command or cue alone. Then transfer to a variable schedule of reinforcement (Fig. 6.9).

The Yield

Teaching the horse to yield his quarters, or move over, is possible using positive reinforcement. If you lure the horse's head round towards you, whilst standing back towards (but not too close to) his hindquarters, you will find that to bring his head to you he will have to move his quarters over. In the beginning reward any sideways movement of the hindquarters away from you, then ask for a larger and more distinct movement as the training goes on. Remember to reward every time the horse tries to yield his quarters until he moves over quickly and in a defined manner. Once the horse will reliably move his quarters, you can add a verbal cue such as 'over' and begin to remove the lure (Fig. 6.10).

Figure 6.10   Sally and Lesley demonstrating the yield.

Training Task: Teaching the Head Down and Placement Using the Target Lure

Teaching the head down can be useful in many situations, e.g. to bridle or halter the horse or if an ear inspection is required. It is also useful to be able to place your horse in a certain area, e.g. a grooming area, and have him stand in place. How to teach both of these skills is explained below using targeting.

The Head Down

Place the target on the floor. The horse should reach down and touch the target. When he reaches down, reward and praise him (even if he does not reach all the way down first time) (Fig. 6.11a). Build up the head-down response until it is reliable enough to add a cue (Fig. 6.11b). Again, remember to switch the horse to a variable reinforcement schedule once the command is established and the target lure is removed.

Placement

A wall-hung target can be used to keep the horse in a position desired by the owner. This is a very good exercise for fidgety horses, especially when you wish to groom, tack up or muck out around them without having to tie them up. If it is necessary to use more than one horse in a training area, a wall target can also help to give one horse a task to do, relieving boredom whilst the other is trained. The wall target can be used to induce stillness and precise placement in the horse. Putting one next to the mounting area or block can also be useful for horses that are wary of being mounted or get excited at the prospect of going for a ride.

Teach the horse to touch the wall target in the same way as you would a hand-held target. Repeat the task until there is a reliable response and then add the cue you wish to use to tell the horse to go to the target. The time the horse remains at the target can then be slowly built up and rewarded on a variable schedule of reinforcement.

Figure 6.11a   Soli learning to do the 'head down' through targeting the end of a schooling stick.

Figure 6.11b   Soli having learnt the cue for head down, which in this case is me pointing down.

MY TRAINING LOG

Here is a place to record your training, experiences and observations. Any notes which might help your future training or your horse as an individual can also be written down to help you. If you have more than one horse or wish to use the table in the future it can be scanned and printed out.

Skill to train	Date Started	Notes	Date Finished
The back			
The heel			
The stay			
The recall			
The yield			
The head down			
Targeting			

Knowing Your Horse: A Guide to Equine Learning, Training and Behaviour
Emma Lethbridge
9781405191647

The Sound of Learning – Clicker Training

Recently, clicker training has become a more popular technique for training horses, although it has been used for many years to train dogs and several other species. Like many of the training techniques based on scientific 'learning theory', clicker training can be generalised for use in training many species of animal (with a little adaptation so that it works most effectively for that species' particular learning ability). Training using the clicker can be very effective and rewarding for the horse and owner, but only if it is applied in an educated and structured way. Clicker training offers a fun way to train, based on positive reinforcement. The following guide will explain how to apply clicker training in an efficient and successful manner.

WHAT IS CLICKER TRAINING?

Clicker training is an operant conditioning training technique. To recap, operant conditioning was first developed by B.F. Skinner (1938) and is a behaviourist theory of learning. It is a form of learning during which an association is formed between a particular behaviour and a consequence. The consequence of the behaviour determines the probability of that behaviour reoccurring. Thorndike's Law of Effect states that if the consequence of the behaviour is undesirable, the behaviour will decrease and if the consequence of a behaviour is desirable, the behaviour will increase in its probability of reoccurring.

An example of operant conditioning at work: if a horse is pawing the ground and the owner gives him a treat, the horse is more likely to paw the ground in the future because he received a positive outcome from the behaviour. Conversely, if the horse paws the ground and accidentally bangs his leg on a wall, he is less likely to paw the ground in the future because this outcome was undesirable.

Where Does the Clicker Come In?

The clicker is a small device which, when pressed, makes a sharp 'click' noise. It was initially a children's toy, before it was discovered to be an extremely useful training device. The clicker acts as a 'conditioned reinforcer'. A conditioned reinforcer is an initially meaningless stimulus, such as a noise or signal, which when associated with a reinforcer, such as food, becomes meaningful to the horse. The click sound of the clicker, once paired with the arrival of food (an innately exciting, primary reinforcer), signals to the horse that his behaviour is correct and he will be rewarded. Although the click itself is not rewarding to the horse, its meaning to the horse is significant (it is conditioned) and lets the horse know that he is performing the correct behaviour.

The clicker is basically a very effective way of saying 'well done' when the horse performs a desired behaviour or an approximation to the desired behaviour. The click ensures that he knows the exact moment he has preformed the correct behaviour and the exact behaviour for which he will be rewarded, and thus he is more likely to repeat that behaviour in the future.

Although other sounds can be used, the click sound is most popular with trainers because it is a very distinctive sound (unlike voice commands which are harder for the horse to pick out amongst the barrage of other words used by us human types).

The clicker is also more practical for distance work, when it is impossible to directly reward the horse with a treat. The clicker enables the gap between the correct response and the reward to be bridged, so that the horse still knows that he is performing the correct behaviour, even if he has to wait a while for the reward.

Does the Secondary Reinforcer Always Have to be a Clicker?

The secondary reinforcer does not have to be a click from a clicker but it does have to be a distinctive sound that is clear to the horse and unlike any other sound used in the horse's training. A downwards 'cluck' of the tongue (which sounds different from the mouth click-ing often done by horse trainers to encourage forward movement) can be extremely useful, especially during riding, long reining and any ground work where both hands are full. I have personally found that this downwards cluck is just as effective as a click from a clicker. However, it is useful to begin with a clicker to establish the structure of clicker training in the minds of both the horse and the trainer.

Words and hand signals can also be used as secondary reinforcers, although they are harder to apply in a way that is understandable to the horse, as they tend to be less distinctive than a click. The word 'Good' could be used or a hand signal such as a 'thumbs up'. If using any of these secondary reinforcers, ensure that the horse under-stands their meaning. You can check if the horse understands the connection between the secondary reinforcer and the coming reward by making the noise; if the horse responds by looking inter-ested or looking for the reward then the meaning of the sound or signal is understood. However, if the horse does not react to the noise in any predictable manner, then it is unlikely that he understands that the secondary reinforcer means that the reward is coming.

These secondary reinforcers are applied in exactly the same way as the clicker training and so, through the rest of the chapter, I will explain the application of the clicker, but keep in mind that the click can be replaced by another sound or signal, if necessary.

The Effect of Secondary Reinforcers such as the Clicker on Learning

Whether clicker training has an effect on the acquisition of a new response or the extinction of it is unclear. A study by McCall and Burgin in 2002 found that a secondary reinforcer, once taught, might facilitate learning when compared to positive reinforce-ment without the secondary reinforcer. In phase 1 of the study the horses were taught to press a lever for food; in this phase one group was rewarded simply with the food and the other was given a secondary reinforcer (a buzzer sound) before the reward. In phase 2 the lever was removed and the horses were taught to push a flap instead for reward. The horses trained using a secondary reinforcer achieved more correct pushes of the flap. There was no difference in the extinction time of the responses. However, this result was different from a study by Williams *et al.*

(2004) which found no significant difference between the horses trained in the study with simple positive reinforcement and those trained with the clicker as a secondary reinforcer signalling arrival of positive reinforcement. Again, there was no difference in the time it took the learned responses to become extinguished.

So clicker and other secondary reinforcer training may or may not facilitate faster learning. However, secondary reinforcers are still highly useful and efficient for training circumstances where the positive reinforcement cannot be delivered swiftly enough otherwise to reward the correct behaviour.

Applying Clicker Training

Figure 7.1 explains the basic routine of applying clicker training.

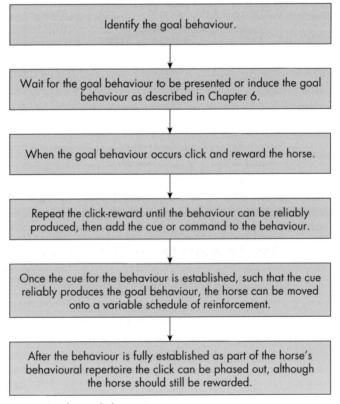

Figure 7.1   Applying clicker training.

Starting Clicker Training

Before you start clicker training, make sure you have the right equipment. Good basic tools to start you off are:

- a bumbag for holding your treats in a contained and easy to reach fashion
- small, palatable and healthy rewards for the horse
- a clicker, which can be attached to your wrist via a wrist strap or to your bumbag to prevent dropping it
- a target (for the horse to touch), which can be anything from a fly swat to a plastic sieve.

THE TRAINING GAME

Before you start clicker training with your horse, here is a fun and very enlightening game to play with a friend (of the human variety) that is recommended by several well-known clicker trainers. The game will consist of the 'trainer', your friend, teaching you, the 'horse', simple tasks using the clicker. Easy, you may say! However, during this game you and your friend are not allowed to communicate verbally. The only communication the trainer can use is the 'click' of the clicker, to let you know when you are doing well and getting closer to performing the correct task. Once the correct task is performed the trainer should clap, to signal the end of the game. The 'horse' must obviously not know what the task is before you start. The trainer should choose a simple task to start off with. Then progress to harder tasks, after a couple of goes.

The point of this game is to allow you to experience clicker training from a horse's point of view. The horse does not know what your desired task is, he has to work purely from the guidance of the clicker which, if not correctly timed, can be confusing. Pretending to be a horse being clicker-trained allows you to experience just how frustrating it can be, trying to figure out what you should be doing. It will also help you to identify what qualities, from the point of view of the horse, make a good trainer, i.e. the timing and frequency of the clicks.

Once you have tried this a few times, switch with your friend, so that you are the trainer. Think of a simple task and, without telling your friend 'the horse' what it is, try and train her to do it. Use only the sound of the click to communicate with her that she is getting closer to the performing the task. Again, once the correct task is performed you, 'the trainer', should clap to signal the end of the game. Practising training in this way allows you to get a feeling for the timing of the clicks. If you get it right, 'the horse' should progress toward the task steadily; if your timing is wrong you will end up with a very confused 'horse'. If your 'horse' seems confused, remain patient and try and be more accurate with your clicks, so that it is easier for the 'horse' to understand what you're asking.

Simple training tasks to begin with would be trying to train someone to sit on a particular chair or to pick up and put on a hat. People have set ideas about how to use objects due to their experience and culture so it is relatively easy to train people to manipulate objects in a manner that is familiar to them in the game. Harder training examples could require the trainer to teach the trainee to pick up the chair or to stand on the hat. To a great extent this premise also applies to objects that horses are familiar with. Training humans may seem silly, but it is an invaluable learning experience and will help you make a better start when you train your horse.

TARGET TRAINING

A good, simple first task to teach your horse is touching a target with their nose. Targeting is taught using clicker training, in a similar way to how it is taught to the horse when using positive reinforcement.

To start teaching the horse to target, hold the target directly in front of the horse's nose. Because horses are naturally curious, the horse will most likely touch the target with his nose. At this moment, click the behaviour and reward with a treat. Repeat this task several times, rewarding each correct target with a click and treat. Once the targeting response is reliable, introduce the target command by saying 'target' as the horse's nose hits the target. As the horse gets used to the targeting task, move the target further away and into different positions, so that the horse has to stretch for it.

Occasionally, the horse will not touch the target, either because he is uninterested or nervous of it. In this situation, click and reward the horse if he turns towards or moves to the target. Keep rewarding the horse as he gets closer to and, eventually, touches the target. Then progress as stated before. Horses should enjoy this task and will quickly understand the role of the click.

Some horses will try to go directly to the bumbag for food. Why work for the food when you can have it straight from the source? If this happens, ignore the horse. Never reward mugging behaviour, otherwise the horse will continue to mug you for food. He will soon learn that the only way to receive the reward is to try the task.

THE SECRETS OF CLICKER SUCCESS

Timing

The click is short in duration, so can be used very precisely to mark the exact moment the desired behaviour occurs; it is far faster to use the clicker than to say 'good horse'. This is important because the horse needs to know exactly which behaviour was correct. If the conditioned reinforcer is too slow, for example a voice stimulus of 'good boy Neddy', the horse won't know whether the correct behaviour was the 'picking his foot up nicely' or the 'slamming it down on to the floor' which occurred a second later, while the verbal secondary reinforcer was being given.

The timing of the click is important. For strongest effect, the click must happen immediately the desired behaviour occurs; even a second too late and the wrong behaviour could be reinforced. The closer the click is to the desired behaviour, the less the chance for confusion in the horse as to which behaviour he is supposed to be performing.

The Filly that Learnt to Flick

An amusing anecdote, which relates perfectly to the importance of the timing when using the clicker, involves a good friend of mine and her new filly. This filly had a habit of flicking her hooves out in a kicking fashion when asked to lift them off the floor. My friend decided to use the clicker to teach her filly to pick her hooves up nicely when asked. Unfortunately, whilst doing this, my friend accidentally 'clicked' when the filly was starting to flick her hoof out. This went on and due to the effectiveness of clicker training, within a few sessions my friend had successfully trained her filly to flick her legs when she asked for her hoof. Thankfully an easily fixed mistake by simply clicking and rewarding only when the filly had raised her leg and was holding it still in a calm fashion.

The moral of the story is this: timing is crucial when using the clicker.

The timing of the reward in comparison to the click is another important factor. At the start of training, the click and treat must be presented to the horse in close proximity to each other, thus producing the association between the clicker and the reward. It is this association which gives the click meaning to the horse. After repetition of the click–reward, the horse will begin to realise that the click signals the imminent arrival of the food reward for the behaviour that was being performed. The click has thus gained meaning to the horse, it means 'well done, you will be rewarded'. Once the meaning of the click is understood by the horse, the period of time between the click and reward can be longer and more variable. This longer waiting period is required for distance work, such as lunging. Furthermore, the number of clicks before the reward can be increased and performed on a variable schedule of reinforcement. If the horse's performance decreases when the waiting period is longer or the number of clicks before the reward is variable, it is likely that he did not understand the meaning of the click. However, in my experience, horses adore clicker training and pick up the concept of the click extremely fast.

Once the desired behaviour is fully embedded in the horse's behaviour repertoire, the click can be phased out. Remove the click gradually, whilst still rewarding the behaviour variably. The click is not for life, it is just for teaching. However, if the click is removed too soon the horse's performance will decrease.

Identifying Goal Behaviours

Before you start teaching a new task to your horse, make sure you have identified exactly what your goal behaviour is. This will help structure your training and ensure that no confusion inhibits your training. It can even be helpful to write your goals down.

Reward the Try

It bears repeating that, as stated above, you make sure that you don't ask the horse to make too large a step in the training. The horse should always be able to succeed in what you are asking of him and you should not ask for too much. Reward each step that is a near approximation of the goal behaviour. Breaking the goal behaviour down into smaller tasks in this fashion will ensure not only success for the horse, but also a quicker arrival at the goal behaviour, as the task is more likely to be understood. Rewarding the try, or shaping, will be discussed in more depth in Chapter 11.

Type and Size of Reward

The food reward should be small, palatable treats. Pony nuts, small bits of apple/carrot and the occasional mint are good rewards. The rewards should be small enough that no training time is wasted on chewing, as this tends to interrupt the flow of a session. Smaller treats are also desirable because as the horse gets fuller, he will be less inclined to work. Smaller treats will fill him up more slowly, making longer training sessions possible. It is an idea to carry more than one type of reward as this keeps an element of surprise for the horse, increasing his desire to work; even the most palatable treat will get boring if used repetitively.

Jackpotting

Again, to recap, if the horse gives a response during the clicker training session which is a particularly good example of the desired behaviour, giving a larger or more exciting reward can increase the chances of getting a good response the next time. Make sure that jackpots don't occur too often or they will lose their effect; save them for the really good efforts.

Introducing Commands and Cues

Commands should be introduced in clicker training exactly as described in Chapter 6. To recap on the important points when introducing commands. . . .

- Always say commands in a higher pitched and friendly voice, which is more appealing to the horse and will separate commands from the rest of your speech, helping the command to be established faster. Never use a stern voice, as this can sound like scolding and is unnecessary; it will also not encourage your horse to work for you.
- Use words which you haven't overused around your horse, for example using 'stay' which is less common than 'stand' when training your horse to stand still.

- Only say the command once so that it is precise and distinct. Repeating the command will not make it clearer to the horse, and may result in him expecting to be told more than once, before he performs the behaviour.
- Signals can be taught just as easily as voice commands and are often clearer to the horse.
- Try and make the commands for each behaviour as different from each other as possible, so that the training is very clear.

Important tips for introducing cues:

- Make sure the cue is clear to the horse. Although the cue itself doesn't have to be large, it has to be distinguishable to the horse.
- Make sure the cue is a movement that the horse does not see from you unless you want that particular behaviour. If the cue is ambiguous the response will not be as good as it would be with a clear cue.
- Again, try to only give the cue clearly, once.
- Make sure the cue is visible to the horse. Although this sounds obvious it is surprising how inaccurate peripheral vision is in both humans and horses, so avoid giving cues in this area if possible, or make them very distinct. Also remember the horse has some blind spots (see Fig. 6.5).

Sessions

At first keep sessions short and structured. Make sure that you don't ask too much of your horse, remember he is new to this too. I usually find that 20 minutes is plenty of time for a first clicker session. During longer sessions, remember to give the horse breaks of either play or rest, depending on his mood, so that he does not become overworked, physically or mentally. The horse should finish the session eager to work; this will ensure that he regards his time with the trainer as a fun and interesting part of the day, to be looked forward to and enjoyed.

Keep it Interesting

Be sure to vary your tasks. Even the most exciting task will become boring if done for too long. If your horse seems to be losing interest, switch to another task; this will maintain his desire to work for you and refresh his mind and movement.

LEARNING RECAP

Reiterating the key points of the chapter and the most important concepts to understand to make your training as successful as possible.

Key Terms	Recap of Definition and Important Concepts
Secondary reinforcers	These are stimuli that have become associated with rewarding stimuli and thus have been conditioned to be rewarding for the horse. The 'click' is a secondary reinforcer.
Timing	The 'click' must occur whilst the behaviour is occurring in order to tell the horse exactly when he is producing the correct behaviour.

Training Task: Using Clicker Training

A Starting Point

All the basic commands, i.e. recall, stay and back, explained before using positive reinforcement, can be also taught using clicker training. Use the click to mark when the horse is doing the desired behaviour and then reward.

However, here are some easy clicker tricks you can train for fun. The point of teaching the horse these tricks is not only for fun, but also to ensure two things.

1. That the horse and handler understand the training system and can communicate effectively within it, that is, the handler

has good timing regarding when to reward and/or click, and the horse understands the role of the click during training.

2. Teaching what seems like silly tricks actually trains the horse how to learn from the click and solve problems (similar to a human perfecting maths, English or metal-working skills), so that he is mentally prepared when asked to perform harder tasks, such as lateral work during dressage, manoeuvring around gates out hacking, or lengthening and shortening his stride during show jumping. These tricks help everyone to improve their performance and enjoyment of training.

Everything we ask our horses to do is a trick, from having a halter put on, to jumping a fence, or performing a piaffe. These are simply fun ones to start clicker training with your horse.

Smile

The smile is a simple trick you can teach your horse. Encourage the horse to move or lift his top lip by wiggling your fingers at his top lip, click and reward when the lift is performed. Then ask for larger, more defined lifts for the click–reward. The cue can be a simple waggle of the fingers (Fig. 7.2).

Figure 7.2   Saffy demonstrating the smile.

Copying – Leg Crossing and Leg Raising

This is a good exercise to encourage the horse to watch and observe your movements as a cue for his own. Improving the horse's observation of your movement can be very useful when it comes to teaching him to observe very light aids in ground work and riding. The horse needs to be focused and in tune with the handler for training to be at its best. The easiest way to teach the horse to observe the handler is to teach him to follow the handler's leg movement.

Teaching the horse to cross his legs is the easiest one to do. Simply encourage the horse to cross his legs as you cross yours. Often a tickle on his upper leg will induce this behaviour. Click and reward when the horse tries the behaviour. Repeat until the horse realises that you crossing your legs is the cue for him to cross his legs (Fig. 7.3). This will require some problem solving from the horse, so be patient.

Leg lifting is taught in a very similar manner. Encourage the horse to lift his leg with yours. This can be done by a tickle on the cannon bone of the lower leg (with a stick if you can't reach but never hit the legs) and then lifting your leg as he lifts his. Click and reward the horse for any attempt at the correct behaviour. Then repeat until the horse understands the connection between you

Figure 7.3   Saffy demonstrating the synchronised leg crossing.

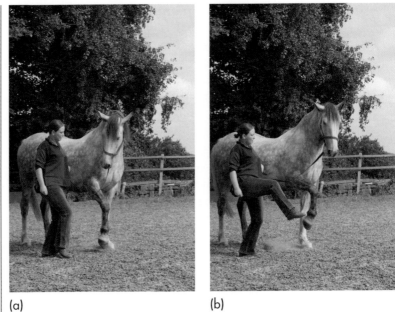

(a)   (b)

Figure 7.4a,b   Saffy demonstrating the leg lift.

(a)   (b)

Figure 7.5a,b   Saffy demonstrating the shoulder-in: in-hand and under saddle taught with clicker training.

lifting your leg and him lifting his and receiving the reward. Start with only a small lift and then accentuate the movement into a larger lift (Fig. 7.4).

However, clicker training is not just for easy tricks, it can be used throughout training. From happy hacking, to high school dressage and jumping, secondary reinforcement training, such as clicker training, can be an invaluable tool. It provides us with an exact way of marking when the desired behaviour occurs and consequently improves our ability to communicate with the horse. Furthermore, secondary reinforcement training offers a way to introduce positive reinforcement into situations where purely primary reinforcement would be tricky to apply, i.e. during distance work (long-lining, lunging and free schooling) and under saddle (Fig. 7.5).

MY TRAINING LOG

The only limits to what you can train using the clicker are the limits of your imagination. This training log is left blank so you can experiment with teaching your horse different tasks and not limit yourself to those described in this chapter.

Skills Trained Using Clicker	Date Started	Notes	Date Finished

Knowing Your Horse: A Guide to Equine Learning, Training and Behaviour
Emma Lethbridge
9781405191647

Negative Reinforcement – Reinforcement Through Escape

To recap, negative reinforcement is simply the removal of an unpleasant or undesirable stimulus in the horse's environment in consequence of a desirable behaviour occurring. The removal of the undesirable stimulus in response to a behaviour encourages that behaviour to reoccur. Negative reinforcement can be useful in horse training. However, it can also be applied in a manner that can be detrimental to both the training and welfare of the horse. To apply negative reinforcement see Fig. 8.1.

Much of current horse training relies on negative conditioning, such as the example given previously of the use of the head collar. When leading the horse, if he starts pulling towards a tasty-looking morsel of grass pressure will be put on the halter, an unpleasant stimulus. When the horse changes his behaviour, stops pulling and

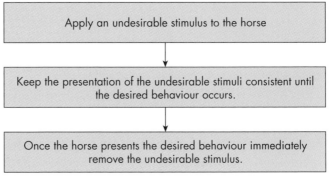

Figure 8.1 Applying negative reinforcement.

begins following the owner, the pressure will be released, removing the unpleasant stimulus. The horse learns that by following the owner he can release and prevent the pressure on the halter.

Many other aspects of horse training are also taught using negative conditioning. The aids for riding, for example, are often taught using negative conditioning. An example of this is when the reins signal the horse to stop, by holding a constant pressure until the horse is still and then the pressure is released. This holding of pressure is unpleasant for most horses and thus the release of the pressure allows the horse to escape the unpleasant stimulus by standing still, reinforcing the standing still behaviour.

A negative reinforcer is any stimulus that is unpleasant to the horse and can be removed from the situation on production of the desired behaviour, increasing the chances of the behaviour reoccurring. Unpleasant stimuli include pressure, painful stimuli and loud noises although ethically, only a non-distressing pressure should ever be used in training.

PRESSURE-RELEASE TRAINING

Pressure-release training is a form of negative conditioning which has become very popular, especially with the recent development of many different types of control head collars. Pressure-release training works on the grounds of application of negative reinforcement (Fig. 8.2).

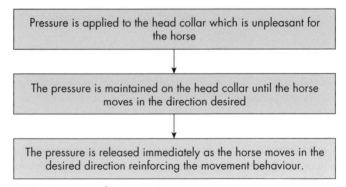

Figure 8.2 Pressure release training.

IMPORTANT FACTORS FOR APPLYING NEGATIVE REINFORCEMENT ETHICALLY

Is the Release of the Adverse Stimulus a Reward?

It is important to note that the release of an adverse stimulus is not that same as a reward. Although both encourage the desired behaviour to reoccur, they are different in the way in which they cause the behaviour to reoccur and their motivational properties. The horse that is rewarded and trained with positive reinforcement works to get his reward, whereas the horse trained with negative reinforcement works to identify the behaviours which cause the adverse stimuli to cease or to prevent the adverse stimuli occurring at all through avoidance learning. For example, when training the horse to yield his quarters through pressure-release, a pressure would be held and then released when the horse moves in the direction required. The pressure is uncomfortable for the horse and the release is reinforcing, so the horse learns that to release the pressure he must move over and after several repetitions, when he sees the owner moving towards his hindquarters, the motivation is to avoid as much of the adverse stimulus as possible. However, if the horse is trained using rewards by encouraging him to yield via luring or targeting, he works to achieve the reward rather than to avoid an unpleasant stimulus or an escalation in unpleasantness. The confusion between the release of the adverse stimulus in negative reinforcement and the reward in positive reinforcement is a common and understandable one but it is important not to confuse the two learning types during training.

How Unpleasant Is Too Unpleasant?

Once I was unfortunate enough to witness someone trying to perform negative reinforcement by pinching the horse's neck until the horse stood still, then releasing the pinch so the horse could escape the pain. However, the horse was terrified of the handler's pinching and obviously would not stand still in such an aroused state, and because of this the pinching would not cease. A vicious circle was occurring because the horse rarely stood for even a second, the pinching didn't stop, and the more fear the horse felt the less he was likely to stand. This could be argued to be very excessive use of force and detrimental to not only the horse's learning but also his welfare.

Furthermore, it is an extremely poor use of a form of learning which can be useful if applied with sensitivity, accuracy and in the right context, all of which the above scenario lacked.

But how do you tell when an adverse stimulus is excessive and possibly even detrimental to the training? The following are the factors I would consider to be indicators of whether the pressure is too much:

- Is the horse fighting or resisting the stimulus? If he is, then the stimulus is most likely too strong and the horse is frightened and thus trying to escape.
- How much discomfort does the horse seem to be experiencing? If the horse appears to be in any form of heightened discomfort or pain, the stimulus is much too strong and could be considered detrimental to the horse's welfare.
- Does the horse seem fearful? Fear is detrimental to the learning process and will therefore decrease the horse's performance.

If the horse seems calm and happy then it is likely that the stimulus isn't too unpleasant. If a stimulus is strong enough that the horse becomes obviously upset or in discomfort, then ethical questions must be raised about the appropriateness of the stimulus, whether there are potentially better methods of training that could be utilised, and whether the ends justify the training means. I always believe that there is a more effective and more appropriate training technique available, such as positive reinforcement or counter con-ditioning, and that to resort to methods involving significant pain or fear is not necessary.

Side Effects of Negative Reinforcement

If the stimulus becomes too unpleasant or the technique is inappro-priate there can be side effects, including the following.

- Panic, due to fear of the unpleasant stimulus, which can result in injury to handler or horse, or both. Even if injury is avoided, panic is certainly detrimental to the horse's ability to learn and his relationship with the handler.
- Aggressive reactions from the horse. If the horse feels trapped by the unpleasant stimulus, occasionally the other side of the fight/flight response will surface and the horse will become

aggressive, although the aggression is still the result of fear caused by an inappropriate or excessive stimulus. Again aggressive responses can result in injury and break down the horse's learning process and/or his trust in his handler.

- Selective reinforcement: the desired behaviour will only occur with certain people, certain equipment such as pressure halters or certain situations, especially if the training is only implemented by certain people, with certain equipment or in certain places.
- Learning can be inhibited by pain or fear in training and these should be avoided for most effective training.

Pain or Fear Can Inhibit Learning and be Detrimental to Training

A study by Rubin *et al.* (1980) trained 15 ponies to jump a small hurdle when a buzzer was sounded; jumping the hurdle allowed the ponies to avoid a mild electric shock. The ponies were split into three groups of five and they trained and received ten learning trials a day. The first group were trained once a week, the second group twice a week and the third group were trained seven days a week. The study found that the ponies who were only trained once a week achieved a high rate of correct responses and learned the training criteria in fewer sessions than those trained seven days a week. In a follow-up experiment the ponies were trained to back up a certain distance to avoid an electric shock. Again they were trained once, twice or seven days a week. This experiment also found that the ponies trained once a week learned the criteria in fewer training sessions.

This experiment, although unpleasant in its design, does demonstrate that the more fear, stress and pain involved in training, the less effectively the training will be as the horse's learning abilities will be reduced. For most effective learning, fear, stress and pain should not be used as part of horse training.

Timing the Release

It is the release of the unpleasant stimulus that teaches the horse. The release must therefore coincide exactly with the presentation of the desired behaviour. The close relationship between the behaviour and the release of the aversive stimulus conditions the behaviour to occur again in response to the stimulus. If the release is too early or late the horse will not understand exactly which behaviour removed the unpleasant stimulus. He may even attribute it to a different behaviour to the one desired and that behaviour will become incorrectly reinforced by the handler.

There are a couple of side effects that can occur if negative reinforcement is used incorrectly. The most important of these to be aware of is 'learned helplessness'. Learned helplessness is caused by the negative stimulus either not being released at all or being released as a random occurrence as perceived by the horse. This randomisation of the release of the unpleasant stimulus causes the horse to believe that there is no way for him to release the stimulus and that all attempts to escape the pressure are futile. As such, the horse becomes shut down and ceases to try and respond to the negative stimulus. Horses which drag behind on the lead rope and don't respond to the pressure of the leader are a good example of this effect, as they have learned they are going to be dragged regardless of their response (although there are other ways this dragging behaviour can be acquired by the horse) and, therefore, the horse stops trying to respond to the leader's pressure and allows himself to be dragged everywhere.

If negative conditioning is not applied lightly, accurately and with absolutely no excessive force, it is often possible for the horse to become desensitised to the unpleasant stimulus and therefore stop reacting to it and learning from the release. Horses which develop hard mouths have often (but not always) fallen victim to poorly applied negative conditioning. The pulling stimulus used on the mouth is often applied too strongly for too long, or despite the horse not responding to it. As such the horse does not understand to stop and the nerves of the mouth become damaged and inactive, failing to respond to pressure stimulus from the reins. However, it is possible to correct a desensitised mouth with correctly applied training, teaching that the reins are a cue to stop, not a physical force used to pull the horse into a stop.

To minimise the chances of the horse becoming desensitised to the unpleasant stimulus, ensure that the stimulus is applied as lightly as will cause a reaction in the horse. Never use excess force and never gradually build up the pressure as this will ensure desensitisation. If the horse does not respond to a comfortable stimulus consider the other training options available.

> **Tip**: It is the release that teaches. The release must occur as soon as the desired behaviour from the horse occurs.

WHEN NOT TO USE NEGATIVE CONDITIONING

Negative conditioning can be ethical and effective as part of a training plan if used with consideration for the horse, lightness and accuracy of stimulation. However, there are occasions when certain stimuli used in negative reinforcement may not be appropriate. Horses are all individuals and respond differently to different stimuli presented to them. This must be taken into account when training. If a stimulus used for negative reinforcement, e.g. pressure, has to be applied with such force that it causes pain or a significant amount of discomfort for the horse, a different training solution should be sought and negative reinforcement not used.

Should the horse be adverse or unreactive to certain forms of stimuli, such as pressure, in these circumstances it is important to be flexible enough in your training to transfer to a different stimulus or method of training, which better suits that individual horse. For example, some horses are oppositely responsive to the pressure of the head collar, backing into it rather than following it. The horse has either learned to behave in this manner because he has misunderstood the meaning of the pressure or he naturally responds in this manner to pressure. This behaviour, despite its varying possible causes, must be dealt with using other training methods, such as positive reinforcement. These horses are poor candidates for pressure-release training, as they will not respond well to pressure. They can, however, usually be taught to move around very effectively using positive reinforcement training with targeting and learning how to move with humans. It is also occasionally possible to find a horse that doesn't respond to pressure, or other stimuli usually considered adverse, because he doesn't find it unpleasant and as such will not respond to the stimulus if it is used as in negative reinforcement context. Again, these horses can be trained effectively using a different stimulus or a different training technique.

AVOIDANCE LEARNING

During training with negative reinforcement, a phenomenon known as avoidance learning will occur. To recap, avoidance learning occurs when the horse predicts the negative stimulus and reacts to prevent it occurring. For example, after the horse understands the concept of pressure-release training and moves with the handler to release the pressure reliably, the horse will begin to move with the handler when they move, without the need for pressure. This is because as the handler moves away, the horse predicts the coming aversive stimulus (the pressure) and moves with the handler to avoid it. This effect is often termed refining the aid, although it is avoidance by the horse which makes the aid seem light.

This avoidance response can be useful during training and should be aimed for by every trainer using negative reinforcement, in order that the aversive stimulus (i.e. pressure), needed for negative reinforcement to be successful, can be stopped. It should, however, be noted that the horse is still only participating in the training and complying with the handler in order to avoid aversive stimuli.

IS EVERY PHYSICAL CONTACT WITH THE HORSE NEGATIVE REINFORCEMENT?

The answer to this is simply 'no', there are plenty of times when aids and physical touch cues are not negative reinforcement. In order for a physical contact with the horse to be negative reinforcement, it has to fulfil two criteria. First, the contact must be aversive to the horse, so that the release of the contact has a benefit to the horse and encourages the behaviour that the release coincided with. Not all physical contact with the horse is aversive to him; in fact, many horses seem to enjoy the majority of gentle human contact. Which type of contact the horse finds aversive will depend very much on the horse as an individual. If an aid is not aversive to the horse, then releasing the contact will have no effect on the release behaviour reoccurring. Such aids which are not aversive can be used as directional cues and then the behaviour can be rewarded instead to make the behaviour more likely to reoccur.

Secondly, the contact must be released to encourage a behaviour to reoccur. If the contact is not released the desired behaviour will

not reoccur and the contact is not being used as negative reinforcement. Be aware, though, that constant, undiscriminating aversive contact can cause learned helplessness and the horse will stop
responding to the contact. Therefore, make sure that any contact that
you require the horse to react to, and the horse considers to be aversive, is not applied to the horse in an undiscriminating or prolonged
manner. This is also necessary to protect the welfare of the horse.

COMBINING POSITIVE AND NEGATIVE REINFORCEMENT

Negative reinforcement can be combined with other forms of training,
such as positive reinforcement, to good effect. To combine the two,
simply reward the horse when the behaviour you want is occurring
and you are releasing the aversive stimulus. For example, when
teaching the horse to halt to a seat aid, the rider will tighten their seat
muscles so that their hips no longer move willingly with the horse's
back (usually a very slight aversive stimulus, but not for all horses).
Because the horse cannot move the rider so easily, they will often
slow down and halt. As the horse slows and halts the tightness of the
rider's seat is relaxed, releasing the slight aversive stimulus and
reinforcing the behaviour. However, to make the reinforcing of this
signal strong it is wise to also reward the horse as he halts and
the seat tightness is released. This ensures that, if the seat tightness
happens not to be aversive, the horse still learns to halt.

The combining of positive and negative reinforcement can
strengthen the behaviour and also ensures that the horse is motivated to work for reward, rather than working to remove or avoid
unpleasant stimuli. Having a horse that works for reward and finds
his work pleasurable is necessary for a strong human–horse communication and an enjoyable training relationship.

The Combination of Negative Reinforcement and Positive Reinforcement – The Effect in Training

The effect of combining negative and positive reinforcement has
been investigated by Warren-Smith and McGreevy (2007). They
compared the effect of negative reinforcement and a combination

of positive and negative reinforcement in training the horse to perform a stop from the rein aid. Horses matched for age, sex and breed were placed into two training groups. It was found that all horses learn how to halt. However, horses trained using the combination of positive and negative reinforcement were less likely to throw their heads vertically, were more likely to relax their mouth and lick their lips and were rounder in their outline than horses trained only with negative reinforcement. It was concluded that the combination of negative and positive reinforcement could be very beneficial in the training of horses from a welfare perspective.

Similar findings were discovered in a study by Heleski *et al.* (2008). During the study the effects of negative reinforcement, and the combination of negative and positive reinforcement on training horses to cross a tarpaulin were observed. Thirty four Arabian horses participated in the experiment and all were handled by the same trainer. Half the horses were trained using negative reinforcement by way of pressure and release on the halter as is traditionally using in horse training, and half were trained using the combination of positive and negative reinforcement with the addition of food and verbal praise to the pressure-release training. If the horses did not walk on to the tarpaulin in 10 minutes it was consider that they had not been successful at the task. Nine of the horses failed the task, six of these from the negative reinforcement only group (although this was not found to be mathematically significant). Interestingly, the experimenters found other effects, in that the addition of positive reinforcement to the training made the training safer for the handler and less tiring as less pressure was needed on the halter.

ADDING CUES AND COMMANDS

Cues and commands are added to negative reinforcement in a very similar manner to how they are added to positive reinforcement behaviours. To recap: the cue or command must only be added once the behaviour can be reliably produced. Only add the cue or command when the horse is performing the behaviour you wish to associate the cue or command with. Until the horse understands the association between the cue or command and the behaviour, he will not react to it, as he is not a mind reader and unfortunately neither does he speak English. Finally, make sure that the cue or command is distinct and very clear to the horse.

LEARNING RECAP

Reiterating the key points of the chapter and the most important concepts to understand to make your training as successful as possible.

Key Terms	Recap of Definition and Important Concepts
Negative reinforcement	Negative reinforcement is simply the removing of an unpleasant or undesirable stimulus (e.g. pressure) in the horse's environment in consequence of a desirable behaviour occurring. The removal of the undesirable stimulus in response to a desirable behaviour occurring encourages that behaviour to reoccur because it is beneficial for the horse to escape the unpleasant stimulus.
Avoidance learning	Avoidance learning occurs when the horse predicts the negative stimulus and reacts to prevent it occurring.
Pressure-release training	Pressure-release training is a form of negative reinforcement. The pressure acts as the unpleasant stimulus and as such the release of the pressure is beneficial to the horse. This causes the behaviour, in response to which the release occurred, to more likely reoccur. The repeated association between the release and the behaviour causes the horse to learn that he can escape the unpleasant pressure by performing the desired behaviour.
Combining positive and negative reinforcement	To combine positive and negative reinforcement, simply reward the horse when the behaviour you want is occurring and you are releasing the adverse stimulus. This combines the reinforcements of releasing the unpleasant stimulus and rewarding the horse.

Training Task: Using Negative Reinforcement Through Pressure-Release

Pressure-release is the form of negative reinforcement to most applicable horse training. The pressure acts as the adverse stimulus, and the timing of the release of pressure by the handler teaches the horse the behaviour required to escape the adverse stimulus. The horse can be taught some of the basic commands using negative reinforcement, for example the heel, the back and the yield. Teaching your horse to move away from pressure, if done sympathetically, can be beneficial for the horse and help him adapt easily to his environment, especially as most people will use pressure as their first method when working around a horse. All of the following pressure-release examples can be combined with positive reinforcement in order to make the training even more effective.

The Back

There are two ways you can train a horse to move back using pressure-release training. One is by applying pressure to the horse's nose either with a hand or the head collar and the second is by placing a hand on the horse's chest. Apply a little pressure to the horse's nose, halter or chest and when the horse moves away, release the pressure. Keep in mind that all horses respond to pressure differently. Some horses will move from a gentle pressure, some will move from the mental pressure of the handler walking towards them and others will not move from pressure at all. If the latter applies it is best to apply a different method of training to teach the back. Applying more and more pressure and causing the horse distress, or possibly significant discomfort, is not a pleasant way to train and should be avoided.

If combining pressure-release with positive reinforcement, reward the horse as the pressure is released. The combination of the release and reward will be a very effective way of insuring that the moving back behaviour occurs again. Gradually ask for bigger and more steps backwards and try to lighten the pressure needed to obtain the desired backing response (Fig. 8.3). Once the horse is reliably moving back from a light pressure or no pressure (i.e. has learnt to avoid pressure by moving back), add a command if desired.

(a)

(b)

Figure 8.3a,b   Remmy and Shannon demonstrate the back via a light nose and halter pressure.

The Heel

The heel can be taught in a similar manner using pressure-release training. As you move away from the horse, allow the rope to gradually pick up until a gentle pressure is being applied to the halter. The horse should feel the pressure and step forward at this point. Release the pressure the instant the horse step towards you. If combining pressure-release with positive reinforcement, reward the horse as the pressure is released. Once the horse seems to understand that moving forwards releases the pressure, ask him to follow you for longer periods and at faster paces. A command can be added if desired. You should also aim at the horse eventually following you to a very light pressure, or no pressure at all, once he has learned to move with the handler to avoid pressure. Again, if the horse seems fearful, confused or distressed by the pressure, switch to an alternative training method to teach the heel. A command can be added to the heel behaviour if desired.

The Yield

To teach a horse to yield his hindquarters and move out of the way of the handler, place a little pressure on the horse's hip with the palm of your hand (make sure you stand out of kick range). The pressure on the horse's hip should encourage him to move his quarters away from the handler. The moment the horse moves away from the pressure, release the pressure from the hip (and reward if combining with positive reinforcement). If the horse doesn't understand to move from the gentle pressure on the hip, then try adjusting where or how you are applying the pressure until the horse moves away, but don't increase the pressure to a point where the horse seems distressed or confused. Once the horse understands to move from the pressure, increase the number of steps over that you ask for, until the horse understands to move over from a light pressure. It is useful to add a command such as 'over', once the yield response is obtained reliably.

Lowering the Head

Pressure-release can be used to encourage the horse to lower his head. Put a little pressure on the halter in a downwards direction. This pressure will encourage the horse to drop his head in the

Figure 8.4   Dolly demonstrating the 'head down'.

direction of the pressure. As soon as the horse drops his head remove all the pressure instantly. The release will condition the horse to drop his head when he feels a little pressure on the poll area of the head collar. If the horse is resisting the pressure, it would be wise to use a different method to teach the horse to drop his head, such as targeting (described in the previous chapter), rather than to increase the pressure. A command can be added, such as a point downwards, once the horse reliably lowers his head to the pressure (Fig. 8.4).

MY TRAINING LOG

Here is a place to record your training, experiences and observations. Any notes which might help your future training, or your horse as an individual, can also be written down. If you have more than one horse or wish to use the table in the future, it can be scanned and printed out.

Skill to Train	Date Started	Notes	Date Finished
The back			
The heel			
The yield			
Lowering the head			

Knowing Your Horse: A Guide to Equine Learning, Training and Behaviour
Emma Lethbridge
9781405191647

Understanding Punishment

'Force will never produce anything beautiful, we cannot use force with our horse. We want to show him in the beauty of his natural movements, therefore we have to treat, handle and respect him as our friend. What a friend he can be, horses don't let you down.' (Franz Mairinger, 1997)

Punishment is a very controversial subject, which is often very emotive; thus it is tempting to try to veer away from tackling the issue of whether to use punishment when training the horse. However, in this chapter an attempt will be made to explain punishment, its effects and how to apply it safely and effectively if necessary.

To recap, punishment is any consequence of a behaviour which results in that behaviour being less likely to occur in the future. When a behaviour occurs less often because of punishment, it is said that the behaviour has become weakened.

Punishment can be split into two types; positive and negative punishment. **Positive punishment** is the addition of an adverse stimulus as a consequence of an unwanted behaviour occurring. The addition of an unpleasant stimulus discourages the behaviour from occurring in the future because it is undesirable for the horse. **Negative punishment** is the removal of something good from the horse as a consequence of an undesirable behaviour occurring. The loss of a desired resource discourages the behaviour from reoccurring. It is difficult to apply negative punishment effectively to horses, although on occasion it can be useful.

Both intrinsic and extrinsic forms of punishment exist. **Intrinsic punishment** is an inherent part of the behaviour that is being punished. For example, if a horse touches a fence he knows to be electrified, the subsequent electric shock is an intrinsic part of the behaviour of touching the electric fence. **Extrinsic punishment** occurs following a behaviour, but is not inherently a part of that behaviour. For example, if a horse is shouted at by the handler in response to barging, the shouting from the handler is not an inherent part of the barging behaviour, but applied to the behaviour by the handler.

In addition, punishment can be primary and secondary. **Primary punishment** uses stimuli that are considered naturally punishing, e.g. loud noises. **Secondary punishers** are stimuli that have become associated with adverse stimuli or other punishers. For example, horses that have been struck around the head will often shy away from a raised hand, despite the raised hand having no intrinsic punishing value.

In a natural environment, punishment is part of most animals' lives. For example, if young horses eat poisonous plants and consequently feel ill, the punishment of feeling ill will deter them from eating the plant in the future. The gregarious nature of horses and their desire to live with others of their own kind in a social group mean that horses may also receive punishment from their peers. A common example of punishment within an equine herd is a horse being driven from an alpha horse's personal space, as a consequence of trying to graze too close. However, a dangerous excuse that is often used to justify physical punishment in training is that horses use physical punishment when interacting with each other, so to communicate with them we can emulate their behaviour. This does not justify physical punishment as, being human, we have more humane training and communication options open to us, which are often much more effective and more ethical than physical punishment.

Punishment is scientifically reliable. That is, punishment when applied correctly will effectively weaken those behaviours targeted. So, given that punishment is present as a normal part of the horse's life and is proven as an effective method of behavioural adaptation, why should it not be applied as part of a training routine? Punishment, especially physical punishment, has many side effects which can be detrimental to the horse's mental well-being and potentially ruin a horse's training, if the trainer is not aware of them. As a trainer it is important to acknowledge and understand these side effects in order to use non-physical punishment ethically and effectively.

Physical punishment is, however, not effective or necessary during training and should not be part of a trainer's repertoire.

THE SIDE EFFECTS AND PROBLEMS OF PUNISHMENT

Punishment Teaches Only What Not to Do

During training punishment is often used in order to attempt to get the horse to change his behaviour. However, punishment does not develop other possibly desirable behaviours, it merely reduces the likelihood of the punished behaviour reoccurring. Desirable behaviours must be encouraged with positive reinforcement if they are to occur with predictable reliability; they will not come through punishing the bad behaviours alone. Training strategies which combine positive reward of correct behaviour along with correct and sympathetic punishment of any undesirable behaviours are more effective.

Addressing the Background Issues

Before applying punishment, it is imperative to make sure that the unwanted behaviour targeted for punishment is not being caused by a physical issue (pain) or a strong psychological issue (phobia). Punishing these behaviours can cause conflict for the horse and thus can cause more undesirable behaviours to occur and be detrimental to the horse's training! How to deal effectively with phobias will be discussed in Chapter 12.

Aggressive and Fearful Reactions

Punishment can evoke strong emotional reactions in horses, such as fear or aggression. These reactions are more likely with physical punishment, but can arise due to verbal or 'removal' punishments. Should the horse feel threatened or cornered, this reaction will be exacerbated, something that trainers must be aware of. If the horse is new to a trainer or lacks trust in the trainer, the behaviour can be further exaggerated. In order to avoid these reactions, any punishment applied should be sympathetic to the horse's personality, i.e. how reactive he is, and also to the situation. Punishment can be applied without such reactions, but only if the horse trusts the trainer and the punishment is non-physical and appropriate for the horse and the situation. Correct punishment can prevent aggressive or neurotic reactions.

Punishment Can Promote Aggression

Punishment can, if used incorrectly, promote aggression within the horse. Correcting aggressive behaviour with physical or verbal positive punishment can provoke rather than quash the aggression. This can be especially true if the cause of the behaviour is not addressed. A common example: a horse with a badly fitting saddle may bite his owner when being saddled. If the owner strikes the horse for his expression of pain, without addressing the cause of the behaviour (the saddle), the horse may exaggerate the behaviour and bite the owner harder because his flight/fight reaction has been heightened by the punishment. Promotion of aggression through punishment can also occur if the horse feels threatened by the punishment or the punishment is overly harsh or delivered with anger. Pain-elicited aggression can also be induced if physical punishment is used, because pain also can heighten a flight/fight response and cause stronger aggressive reactions in the horse as he tries to escape the threat of pain.

Learned Helplessness

Learned helplessness is a condition which can be induced through the misguided use of punishment. Learned helplessness occurs when the horse cannot avoid punishment over a period of time. The horse learns that any attempts to escape are futile and enters a state of helplessness in which he will not attempt to escape or avoid the punishment, even if an escape or avoidance method is offered.

The theory of learned helplessness was formulated in 1965 at the University of Pennsylvania by Martin Seligman. Seligman was studying Skinner's behaviourism by conditioning a dog to associate a sound with an electric shock (1960s ethics within scientific animal research were a lot less strict than they are now). He found that contrary to Skinner's theory, when eventually given the option to avoid the shocks, the dogs would not try to escape their punishment. This occurred because they had not been able to escape the shocks for a significant period of time at the beginning of the experiment. Horses can enter a state of learned helplessness in which they will just accept any punishment because they believe that they can't escape it. A common example of a behaviour that resembles learned helplessness in the horse is the riding school horse that will not go forward despite any amount of kicking and hitting from the rider. The horse may have learned that he will get hit and kicked regardless of the behaviour he exhibits. The horse's behaviour may become very constricted through learned helplessness, resulting in an apparently depressed horse.

Avoidance Behaviours

If the horse learns to associate a person or situation with punishment, he may logically try to avoid that situation. For example, should the horse be punished for not standing to be mounted at the mounting block, he may decide that the best way to avoid punishment is to avoid the mounting block. Similarly, if the horse has painful front feet he may find that the act of jumping is punished on landing by pain. Therefore, the horse could learn to avoid jumping by refusing. Trainers and owners must be aware that punishment can cause the horse to avoid certain situations or even people. Understanding of this side effect can help prevent this effect from occurring in the horse's training.

Selective Weakening of Behaviour

It is also possible for horses to selectively suppress the punished behaviour until punishment is less likely, either when the punishing handler is no longer present or when the horse believes that he is less likely to be punished for the behaviour. Often, when one person continually delivers punishment to the horse consistently, the horse will learn to suppress the punished behaviour around that person. However, the behaviour is likely to reoccur with other handlers when punishment is less likely. A good example of this is the horse that is pushy with certain people who do not punish the barging behaviour, but perfectly behaved with those who do punish the same behaviour. This effect is especially likely to occur if the motivation to perform the behaviour outweighs the potential risk of punishment. Trainers and owners must be very aware of this effect, if they are training any horse who is to be handled by more people than just the owner or trainer.

Impairment of Attention

Anxiety caused by punishment can actually impair the horse's ability to concentrate and learn effectively. Extreme emotions inhibit the brain's cognitive abilities and thus impair attention. Exam anxiety is a good human example of this effect. In order to ensure that punishment does not create poor performance in the horse, the punishment must not create a large amount of anxiety or aggression. Physical punishment can potentially cause a lot of anxiety or aggression in the horse and thus must be used very carefully, if at all, to avoid compromising the horse's attention and performance.

Reduced Interest

Punishment used without any positive reinforcement can reduce the horse's interest in his work. If a horse is punished, the motivation for him to perform the task will be diminished and thus he is less likely to participate willingly. This effect is present in both humans and animals. Martin found in 1977 that children have reduced interest in tasks during which they have been reprimanded in the past.

Desensitisation

Knowing at what level to apply punishment is a very sensitive matter and is individual to each horse. If the punishment is too severe the horse will become fearful or possibly aggressive, among other side effects already discussed. However, if the punishment is too mild it will fail to suppress the undesirable behaviour. A common mistake made when applying punishment is that the punishment is too mild so the horse doesn't react. The handler then raises the punishment slightly but the horse still doesn't react, so the handler increases the severity of the punishment slightly, creating a vicious circle. The horse isn't reacting to the punishment because the handler is accidentally systematically desensitising the horse to it. Should the vicious circle continue, the horse will appear to be stubborn by not reacting to the punishment, when in fact the horse is not being stubborn but is acting according to the experiences of punishment he has encountered.

Horses that are insensitive to the crop are often a practical example of desensitisation. It is common practice to strike a horse with a riding crop if he doesn't increase speed in response to the leg aid. However, the horse is usually tapped lightly to begin with and then the strike is increased as the horse doesn't respond to the crop. If the crop is applied in this manner many horses learn to ignore or tolerate the crop, even when it is used with severity. Physical crop use is not necessary during horse training; if the horse is very lazy, it is more ethical and often more effective to use the crop to bang your boot or wave it at the horse. To avoid desensitisation to a punisher such as a noise or movement, a good understanding of the horse's reactivity is necessary, along with the ability to judge the correct level of punishment required to cause a reaction in the horse, but without creating neurosis or aggression. This is very difficult and requires accuracy and sensitivity from the trainer.

APPLYING PUNISHMENT (MINIMISING THE SIDE EFFECTS)

For punishment to be effective and avoid side effects it must be:

♦ immediate
♦ consistent
♦ sufficient in intensity
♦ never used in anger
♦ specific to targeted unwanted behaviours and not delivered randomly or accidentally
♦ never used to punish confusion.

Given that the use of punishment can create undesirable side effects and simply teaches the horse what not to do, but suggests no alternative behaviour, can punishment be used effectively as part of training?

Yes, but it requires skill, timing and sympathy. Physical punishment should be avoided.

Immediate Punishment

The most effective forms of punishment are those that are delivered immediately after the unwanted behaviour. This has the effect of ensuring a strong association between the unwanted behaviour and the punishment. A strong association is necessary for the successful weakening of the undesirable behaviour. If the punishment is delayed or mistimed, the horse may associate the punishment with the wrong behaviour (possibly even with a desired behaviour). For example, if a horse breaks free from the handler and escapes, the handler may chastise the horse once caught. However, by chastising the horse for being caught, the handler is punishing the being-caught behaviour rather than the breaking-free behaviour. The result of such a delayed punishment is that the horse's breaking-away behaviour will not have been affected, but the punishment when caught will understandably have weakened the horse wanting to allow itself to be caught again. This is an extreme example, but a delay of even a few seconds can have profound results on the effect of the punishment.

This rule applies to both negative and positive punishments. Not feeding the horse because he did not perform well during a schooling session will have no effect on his behaviour during schooling sessions, because the delay between the two events is too great. Hence there will be no association between the two. However, removing a potential food reward immediately from a horse who is mugging will suppress the mugging behaviour because of the close temporal association between the mugging behaviour and the removal of the food.

Consistency

For punishment to be completely effective, every incident of the undesirable behaviour must be punished. If only some of the responses are punished, the behaviour will not be fully suppressed. A common example of partial punishment not fully suppressing behaviour is shown by those owners who allow their horses to rub on them some of the time, and possibly even encourage it, but when the owner is in their best clothes or in a bad mood, the horse is punished for the same behaviour. This partial punishment will not suppress the behaviour. Consistency is a key factor in the successful and sympathetic application of punishment. Without consistency the horse may become confused regarding whether certain behaviours are allowed or not.

Sufficient Intensity

So what exactly is 'sufficient intensity'? This is an important question, as intensity is one of the key determinants of whether any attempted punishment will be successful, especially relevant when considering the use of physical punishment. Non-physical punishments are less subject to this question; for example, the negative punishment of removing food can be raised in intensity by removing a more palatable appetizer, but is less likely to cause substantial side effects due to increasing or decreasing intensity.

There are several factors that must be taken into account when judging what intensity of punishment is appropriate for preventing unwanted behaviours. Studies have shown that mild punishments can often be ineffective in weakening behaviours and can, in fact, desensitise the horse to future stronger punishment. However, stronger punishment is objectionable because of the potentially increased pain or anxiety caused to the horse and thus the increased risk of side effects.

This leaves us with a difficult dilemma! Should we punish mildly and possibly end up applying more punishments due to ineffectiveness, and even potentially have to use a higher intensity of punishment than would have originally been necessary due to the horse becoming desensitised to the punishment? Or should we start by using a higher intensity of punishment, with the possible result of having to apply fewer punishments due to greater effectiveness, but risking side effects due to applying too much intensity and causing additional pain/discomfort/anxiety to the horse?

Every horse responds differently to punishment because of both his innate disposition (how reactive the horse is to stimuli, etc.) and his previous experiences of training. When applying punishment, it is essential that the horse's personality is taken into account and thus the punishment is sympathetic to the horse. For example, a very reactive horse or one who has been punished harshly in the past will need very little intensity of punishment in order to suppress undesirable behaviours. However, horses who are not reactive or who have been desensitised by badly applied punishment earlier in the training may require a higher intensity of punishment. Consideration of the horse's individual differences will ensure that the judgement of the intensity at which to apply punishment will be as accurate as possible.

An Answer to the Dilemma of Intensity

It is possible to keep punishment as mild as possible, as long as another desirable behaviour can be encouraged by positive reinforcement to replace it. In this case intensity becomes much less of an issue. The mild punishment serves only to suppress the behaviour long enough to encourage a desired behaviour, and not to suppress the behaviour itself. This strategy may be the most ethical application of punishment and will be discussed in more detail later in the chapter.

Never Punish in Anger

It is imperative to the success of training that any punishment necessary is never dealt out in anger. Anger can easily cause the punishment to be badly applied, causing it to be badly timed or apparently erratic. This in turn causes the punishment to appear to have no associated behaviour, but instead be a series of random adverse events. Additionally, anger is likely to cause the punishment to be dealt out with too much intensity. Both of these factors could become determinants in the development of side effects. Punishment is best applied in a calm and rational manner.

Specific to Targeted Unwanted Behaviours and Not Delivered Randomly or Accidentally

For a training programme to be truly successful, it is crucially important to be very clear about which behaviours you wish to encourage from your horse and those that you consider unacceptable. A precise training agenda will give you clarity within your training and ensure that only those behaviours intended are targeted for punishment. Specifying targeting undesirable behaviours, and having knowledge of how punishment must be applied, will ensure that side effects are avoided as far as possible, and that punishment is not applied accidentally or to the wrong behaviour. For example, decide in advance whether your horse is allowed to rub on you or to search your pockets; this will prevent confusion during training. Being very clear with your intensions is half the battle.

Never Punish Confusion

Often a horse will fail to comply with a command or perform an undesirable behaviour because he is confused as to how to behave or does not understand the handler's directions. This confusion should not be punished. Punishment of such behaviours will only cause the horse to become anxious or resentful the next time he encounters a confusing situation. If you are even slightly concerned that the horse's behaviour may be due to confusion, try not to use punishment, especially not intense or physical punishment. Instead, use another method to deal with the undesirable behaviour (discussed in Chapter 10) or help the horse to understand what you require from him by another training method, such as shaping (discussed in Chapter 11).

An Ideal Strategy for Applying Punishment

Mild Punishment should temporarily suppress the behaviour. No great intensity is needed; simply withholding reward will usually be sufficient negative punishment to suppress the undesirable behaviour. Physical or corporal punishment should not be required. The purpose of the punishment is simply to suppress the behaviour so that it can be **combined with**. . . .

Reinforcement of correct alternative behaviours. Giving the horse an alternative rewarded behaviour will cause him to engage in this behaviour, rather than the punished undesirable behaviour. The horse (like all animals) will engage in those behaviours which he believes are most beneficial for his survival. If we make the behaviours we desire more beneficial for the horse to perform, he will choose to perform these behaviours preferentially. Conditioning desired behaviours in such a manner will ensure that the horse achieves the behaviours desired by the handler, with a vastly reduced risk of encountering side effects, which could be detrimental to the horse or the training.

Unless there is a physical cause (pain) or strong psychological cause (phobia) for the behaviour; then the cause of the behaviour requires addressing.

IS IT POSSIBLE TO TRAIN A HORSE WITHOUT THE USE OF PUNISHMENT?

Yes, it is possible to train without punishment, but it requires a good knowledge of equine learning and behaviour. The application of techniques such as extinction, counter conditioning, desensitisation, shaping and negative reinforcement (all discussed within this book) must be very accurate and, furthermore, the trainer must be able to apply these techniques in novel ways, so as to transform unwanted behaviours into desirable ones. An ideal we should all work towards. However, there is no reason why non-physical punishment should not be used as long as it is applied correctly, and with suitable concern for the welfare of the horse.

LEARNING RECAP

Reiterating the key points of the chapter and the most important concepts to understand to make your training as successful as possible.

Key Terms	Recap of Definition and Important Concepts
Positive punishment	Positive punishment is the addition of an adverse stimulus (e.g. a smack) as a consequence of an unwanted behaviour occurring. The addition of an unpleasant stimulus discourages the behaviour from occurring in the future because it is undesirable for the horse.
Negative punishment	Negative punishment is the removal of something good from the horse (e.g. food) as a consequence of an undesirable behaviour occurring. The loss of a desired resource discourages the behaviour from reoccurring.

cont'd

Key Terms	Recap of Definition and Important Concepts
The side effects of punishment	Potential side effects and problems associated with punishment: • Punishment only teaches the horse what not to do, but offers no alternative behaviour for the horse to engage in • Punishment can induce fear and aggression if badly applied • Badly applied punishment can induce learned helplessness in the horse • The horse may learn simply to avoid the punisher • Punishment can impair the horse's attention and learning • The horse can lose interest in his training • Desensitisation.
Important points for applying punishment safely	For punishment to be applied in a way that is ethical and effective at reducing the unwanted behaviour, it must be: • Immediate • Consistent • Sufficient in intensity • Never used in anger • Specific to targeted unwanted behaviours and not delivered randomly or accidentally • Never used to punish confusion.

How to Deal with Unwanted
Behaviours Without Using Punishment

Often it may seem that punishment is the only option when dealing with unwanted behaviours, especially if the behaviours are inconvenient, annoying or even painful. However, there are ways to stop unwanted behaviours occurring without the need for punishment. Limiting the amount of punishment used within training will ensure that the horse's training is pleasurable for both handler and horse, well communicated and, furthermore, that trust is maintained between horse and handler. Trust is necessary during training in order that the horse can be relaxed and learn efficiently. In order for trust to develop, the horse must feel unthreatened around the owner. Reducing, or even preventing, the use of punishment limits the potential side effects which can be caused by punishment, even if it is well applied, and ensures the best welfare for the horse during his interaction with humans. It is important that any potential causes of the behaviour, which may be pain or management based, are addressed and removed before the behaviour is tackled through training.

THE SIMPLEST AND HARDEST OPTION – IGNORING THE HORSE

If the horse is performing an unwanted behaviour to try and get the handler's attention, or to provoke a reaction, then ignoring him can stop the problem. However, ignoring the behaviour is often easier said than done, especially if behaviour is aggressive or inconvenient. Ignoring the horse works because it stops him gaining the attention he wants. Once the unwanted behaviour has stopped being rein-forced by the reaction of the handler, the behaviour will disappear.

The process of an unwanted behaviour disappearing, due to the reward for the behaviour (i.e. the handler's attention) ceasing, is known as extinction (as discussed in Chapter 5). Extinction is the reduction of a behaviour due to the cessation of a reward. It is the opposite of conditioning – deconditioning if you like. Once the behaviour is not being reinforced, it will gradually disappear from the horse's behavioural repertoire, until it is gone completely. It is imperative during this time that the ignoring of the unwanted behaviour is complete and continuous. Any reinforcement will stop the extinction process and cause the horse to continue to perform the unwanted behaviour. If the behaviour is difficult to ignore whilst continuing what you are doing, walk away from the horse and turn your back to him. This will show the horse clearly that the behaviour is not going to be rewarded.

There are many good examples of unwanted horse behaviours which are usually maintained by the handler's reaction, even if that reaction is negative (I come across many horses who will try to provoke negative reactions from their owners). Nipping (which resembles foal play) is often maintained by the handler's reaction. The handler and the horse get stuck in a vicious circle of the horse nipping the handler, and in response the handler shouting at, slap-ping or pushing the horse. However, the slaps and pushes resemble play and the horse has succeeded in getting the attention of the handler and thus the behaviour is reinforced rather than punished. Ignoring the nipping behaviour will stop the horse being inadvert-ently rewarded for nipping and, therefore, the behaviour will reduce and eventually disappear through the extinction process

Head butting, floor pawing, door banging and rubbing can also be behaviours which are performed to achieve a reaction from the handler and which are maintained by the handler's reaction, although there can be other reasons for the performance of these behaviours.

When Ignoring the Behaviour Doesn't Work

In some circumstances, ignoring the behaviour won't work. These may include:

- If the reason why the horse is performing the behaviour is not the owner's reinforcement of the behaviour, it is unlikely that ignoring the behaviour will make it desist.
- If the stimulus which sets off the behaviour is still present and influential in the horse's environment, the behaviour will continue to be performed regardless of the owner ignoring the behaviour. If the unwanted behaviour is caused by pain or a phobia then it is necessary to deal with the pain or phobia before continuing to train the unwanted behaviour out. Should the cause of the behaviour not be dealt with, ignoring the unwanted behaviour will have little effect.
- However, if the behaviour is due to fear or pain, often heeding (not increasing pressure on the horse to continue the task), but not responding to the horse's behaviour, can increase the trust between the horse and handler and therefore act to reduce the horse's unwanted behaviour whilst the pain is being treated and removed. A lot of horse aggression is fear or pain related. How many horses do you see bite their handlers and then run backwards in fear of the handler? It is, however, imperative that, even if you do not respond to the behaviour, you are safe from the consequences of the behaviour (i.e. don't let the horse bite or kick you).

COUNTER CONDITIONING

Counter conditioning is the fancy term for teaching the horse to perform a behaviour which is incompatible with the unwanted behaviour. The two behaviours must not be able to be performed at the same time by the horse, so that the new behaviour prevents the old unwanted one from occurring. The incompatible behaviour can be taught with positive conditioning and then can be performed instead of the unwanted behaviour. Once the horse has established that he is to perform the counter behaviour (the desired behaviour alternative) and that it is more beneficial to perform this behaviour, i.e. it is rewarded whereas the undesirable behaviour is not, the horse will permanently switch to the counter behaviour.

The 'don't mug me' training is an example of counter conditioning; the horse cannot perform the mugging behaviour and the looking away behaviour at the same time. As the looking away behaviour is reinforced with food rewards, the horse will choose to not mug the handler, because it is more beneficial for him to perform the counter-conditioned behaviour, the looking away. Eventually the counter behaviour will become the behaviour of choice for the horse and take over from the undesirable behaviour permanently.

Another example of unwanted behaviour is fidgeting when having the saddle put on due to excitement because of the imminent work, fear of the coming work, memory of saddle pain or current saddle pain (among other possible causes). If the fidgeting is thought to be due to current saddle pain or fear of work, then the saddle needs to be refitted and the horse's work changed to something he does not fear. Once this has been dealt with, the horse can be counter conditioned to stand still whilst being saddled. Simply hold the saddle near the horse and then when the horse is still and calm, reward him (with a food reward or through clicker training). Repeat until the horse stands for longer periods of time and the saddle is closer. Gradually put the saddle on the horse, rewarding the horse when he is calm and still. The horse should realise that the standing behaviour is much more beneficial than the moving behaviour and switch to this behaviour throughout the saddling procedure. The time it takes to reach this point will vary for each horse, dependent on their personality and their experiences. Once the horse stands still reliably, he can be rewarded on a variable schedule of reinforcement.

Most unwanted behaviours can be replaced by a counter-conditioned desirable behaviour. It is a case of finding an alternative behaviour to reward, in order to show the horse exactly the behaviour you want from him, rather than simply punishing the behaviours you don't want, which doesn't give the horse any guidance as to which behaviours are desired.

DRIVEN TO DISTRACTION

Distraction can be a very useful tool when dealing with unwanted behaviours. An unwanted behaviour can be nipped in the bud by cueing a separate unrelated behaviour such as backing up, touching a target or even something more complicated such as Spanish walk, leg yielding or a turn on the forehand. This action is more effective than punishment as punishment only teaches the horse what you don't want, whereas giving the horse rewardable tasks shows him clearly which behaviours are desired of him.

The distraction allows the horse to engage in a behaviour for which he will be rewarded and to refocus his mind on a task. Often horses will engage in undesirable behaviours if they are tense or unfocused. Giving the horse a task which is achievable and well rewarded will allow him to maintain self-confidence and focus. The distraction task behaviour is not designed to replace the unwanted behaviour in all circumstances, as in counter conditioning, but merely to transfer the horse's energies onto a task which is beneficial to your relationship rather than getting into a battle with the horse over the unwanted behaviour. The aim of distraction is that the horse should eventually only engage in desired behaviours through choice.

For example, if a horse is getting spooky during a training session, often his mind can be easily refocused by distracting him. This can be done by executing a simple transition, a rein back or a lateral exercise. All of these require the horse to adjust his balance and pace and thus require his full attention. Alternatively, if a horse starts to become pushy, bargy or uninterested during training his energies can be refocused by a simple backing up exercise or a task of your choice. A potentially negative or dangerous situation can be turned into a positive and beneficial training opportunity.

This form of dealing with unwanted behaviour is beneficial both because it nips bad behaviour in the bud without the need for punishment, and it shows the horse that there are alternative behaviours which are desired and rewarded. Rather than merely punishing the horse, which gives him no guidance as to an alternative to the unwanted behaviour, distraction gives him a way to receive a reward and succeed during training, encouraging a stronger bond and greater communication between trainer and horse.

When Distraction Is Difficult

There are occasions when distraction is difficult to apply:

- If the horse is in a state of very high anxiety, excitement or fear, then distraction maybe difficult. Horses find it very difficult to concentrate when they are highly aroused. However, distracting the horse and refocusing him can improve his state of mind and encourage him to begin thinking and thus he will begin to calm down.
- If the stimulus which starts the unwanted behaviour is particularly strong and influential in the horse's environment, it will be

difficult to distract him from it. If the unwanted behaviour is caused by pain or a phobia, then it is necessary to deal with the pain or phobia before continuing to train the unwanted behaviour out. Should the cause of the behaviour not be dealt with, the distraction will have little effect.

A FINAL NOTE

The horse never performs an unwanted behaviour knowing that it is unwanted or wrong. Right and wrong are human concepts, not attainable by the horse's mind. The horse simply believes that the behaviour he is performing is the best way to survive in his environment. Although correctly applied punishment would reduce the unwanted behaviour, given the innocent nature of the horse's mind, we owe it to him to find the kindest and most effective method to show him that his behaviour is unwanted and that there are alternative behaviours, which are not only desired by the handler but also more beneficial to the horse and his success in his environment. Many undesirable behaviours are often caused by the horse's fear of an element of his environment. If you suspect fear is the likely cause of your horse's undesirable behaviour, then a guide to how to help your horse overcome his fear can be found in Chapter 12.

LEARNING RECAP

Reiterating the key points of the chapter and the most important concepts to understand to make your training as successful as possible.

Key Terms	Recap of Definition and Important Concepts
Extinction	Extinction is the reduction of a behaviour due to the cessation of a reward. For example, if mugging behaviour is no longer rewarded it should desist, or if the horse no longer receives the attention he wants for ground pawing, the ground pawing would cease.
Counter conditioning	Counter conditioning is teaching the horse to perform a behaviour which is incompatible with the unwanted behaviour, instead of the unwanted behaviour. The two behaviours must not be able to be performed at the same time by the horse, so that the new behaviour prevents the old unwanted one from occurring.
Distraction	By distracting the horse, he may be prevented from performing the unwanted behaviour. A good way to distract the horse is to give him a simple task to do for which he can be rewarded. If the horse is focusing on a task he is less likely to engage in unwanted behaviours, especially if the task is likely to be rewarded.

Case Studies: Alternative Ways to Correct Unwanted Behaviour

Billy – From Demon to Diamond Geeza!

Billy's owner Ross describes the situation – 'Billy was bought at auction as an unhandled two year old. Basics like leading, hoof handling and loading were taught and Billy quickly became a well-mannered youngster who was a pleasure to be with. Shortly after his basic training was completed a local college running a generic animal care qualification took Billy on loan at their open farm.

The farm is open to the public who can purchase small bags of grass nuts to feed the various animals there. Billy was three and a half years old when staff from the college informed us that his behaviour was becoming a problem for them and they wanted to send him back to us. Billy had become dominant and unruly and frequently knocked down fences. He was striking out at people with his front legs and had become aggressive around food. He had little "respect" for his handlers.

Once he had returned the inappropriate behaviour subsided to a degree and we started him under saddle. However, he still displayed dominant behaviour and was very pushy, especially around food. Billy continued to bite and invade our personal space and use his head to knock us around. We made a decision that food rewards would only exacerbate the problems so we kept this option out of his training completely. We decided to explore the possibilities of positive reinforcement and gain further knowledge after reading some books on the subject , so we contacted Emma after a recommendation.

Emma started regular training sessions with Billy and helped us understand the techniques which would work for Billy's personality. Using positive reinforcement very accurately started to teach Billy that he needed to be relaxed and that he would only be rewarded when he was not being pushy. The results were almost instantaneous. His learning was faster than ever before. He was eager to learn and started to reveal what a talented horse he actually was. Billy's personality remains cheeky and fun but he now shares our enthusiasm to learn in a controlled way.'

Solution

Billy had learned that he could receive treats through displaying bolshy behaviour. He had also learned that he could receive any attention he wanted through aggressive behaviours. Billy wished to attract any attention, good or bad, possibly because the attention may have lead to him being able to extract rewards from the person giving the attention or gave him other advantages in his environment. As such, positive punishment is less effective for a horse like Billy because it is usually necessary to interact with the horse to apply it; for Billy, this interaction could encourage the behaviour to continue as he will have achieved the attention he desired and the behaviour would have been reinforced. However, there are other techniques that can be used to tackle nipping and bolshy behaviours.

First, to tackle the problem, the handler must not respond or interact with the horse more than necessary to keep safe when the bolshy behaviour is occurring. This will ensure that the behaviour is not accidentally reinforced by the attention and encouraged to continue. Second, Billy was taught how to behave correctly around food rewards through the no mugging training described earlier in the book. Billy soon realised that only calm and quiet behaviour allowed him access to the food reward. Finally, it was necessary to counter condition Billy's bolshy behaviour so that he learned that quiet, calm behaviour was more rewarding than bolshy or aggressive behaviour and as such, it was more beneficial for him to behave in a safe, quiet manner. Billy cannot act in an aggressive and a quiet manner simultaneously and so rewarding quiet behaviour will cause the extinguishing of the aggressive behaviour.

The counter conditioning was achieved by working through some basic manoeuvres such as backing up and leading, and only rewarding Billy when his behaviour was pleasant and quiet. The manoeuvres were also used to refocus Billy's attention if he started displaying undesirable behaviours such as nipping or pushing. This ensured that Billy was always engaging in behaviours that could be rewarded. After a short period Billy realised that only quietly performing the behaviour requested in a co-operative manner earned him rewards and he became much more amiable to be around. He was also rewarded for any period of time in which he chose to stand still when around the handlers to counter condition the pestering behaviour and extinguish it.

Once this initial training was complete and Billy was behaving in a safe and co-operative manner, the food rewards were slowly reduced and he was put on a variable schedule of reward to ensure the longevity and sustainability of the new safe behaviour. It was also now possible to utilise Billy's intelligence in a more productive manner and move to higher level training using positive reinforcement within training.

The Schooling of Saffy

Lynne tells us about Saffy – 'Saffy is a registered Irish Sport Horse that I bought from a dealer as a five year old in September 2004. Physically she was ewe necked when I bought her as she preferred to work with her neck vertical and her nose in the air which made it very difficult to school her correctly.

In addition to this, she couldn't tolerate a contact on her mouth and would rear when you picked up even the lightest of contacts. She would do this over a dozen times in a session at halt and in walk and trot. Initially I had to take her bitless for three months and then gradually reintroduce her to a bit again. This was partially successful but she was still quite tense in the school and would easily revert back to star gazing. The rearing was much improved, although she would still "spin" and rear on the occasions when she was very tense. Although she was fairly brave out hacking, being happy to take the lead or even go out solo, there were places in the school where she was excessively spooky and at times couldn't be worked due to this.

I looked at her diet and found that taking her off all hard feeds and supplementing with magnesium helped somewhat. I also followed a programme of groundwork which also helped, but neither of these approaches resolved the problem entirely. We introduced clicker training into all aspects of her work, including groundwork, in hand/long reining and under saddle. Using clicker training as part of our everyday handling has improved her attitude and behaviour immensely. She now actively enjoys working and will try much harder than she did before in all aspects of her training. Although she still has the occasional spook, her reactions are greatly diminished and it doesn't spoil the training session in the way that it would have done previously.

Physically she has changed immensely too. Now that she is happier to work and more relaxed in general, her ewe neck has been reversed and she has started to build a correct musculature.'

Solution

Saffy's incorrect way of going was caused by her tension about being schooled and contact on her mouth. Saffy associated schooling with a certain amount of anxiety which caused her to be very unpredictable in her behaviour and to work in a tense fashion with her head very high. This way of going will cause large amounts of stress to be put through the musculature and skeleton of the horse, especially through the back as the abdominal muscles would be disengaged and thus not able to tighten and support the back. In order for us to work on Saffy's biomechanical issues, it was first necessary to work on her unpredictability, spooking and rearing which were all undesirable behaviours.

Saffy was introduced to clicker training so that she could be rewarded for good behaviour under saddle. The clicker training was introduced through groundwork first which encouraged Saffy to start finding pleasure in being in the schooling area. Once she understood the association between the click and the arrival of the food reward, the clicker training was transferred to the ridden work.

During schooling sessions, Saffy's unpredictability was counter conditioned by rewarding calm behaviour with the clicker training. Rewarding the calm behaviour caused Saffy to control her anxiety so that she could receive rewards. Eventually the calm behaviour would become rewarding in itself. More complex schooling movements were also added to Saffy's repertoire, including rein back, direct transitions, basic laterals (leg yield, shoulder in, renvers and travers), turn on the forehand and haunches and pole work. These exercises had three purposes: first, they kept the cognitive parts of Saffy's brain working – this will help to suppress any excessive anxiety. Second, they kept Saffy on task and distracted from outside stimuli – this allows her the chance to earn more rewards for calm desired behaviours, and offers her continuous guidance towards wanted behaviours without ambiguity. Finally, these movements when performed correctly encouraged her to engage her abdomen and relax her back and neck muscles. This helped reduce the tension in Saffy's body and helped her to find schooling easier and start to find pleasure and relaxation in her riding work.

If any undesirable behaviours such as spooking, rearing or tension occurred during training they were ignored and the aids for the task were gently applied until Saffy returned to the task. Once back on task, she was rewarded for continuing the co-operative behaviour. The riding should always be quiet, controlled and firm but never forceful or distressing for the horse.

The combination of clicker training and exercises has helped to create a relaxed horse who is co-operative and enjoys being trained. Saffy is now a safe and pleasant ride and a willing, enthusiastic partner in her training. Biomechanically, she is working in a way that is more beneficial, and her musculature is developing in a strong, correct manner. This will help prevent injury and ensure longevity of her working life.

MY TRAINING LOG – ADDRESSING UNWANTED BEHAVIOURS

If your horse has any undesirable behaviours, such as nipping, here is a place you can record your own and your horse's progress in solving those behaviours using the above techniques.

Behaviour to be Addressed	Date Started	Method Used	Notes	Date Finished

Knowing Your Horse: A Guide to Equine Learning, Training and Behaviour
Emma Lethbridge
9781405191647

Step by Step

When teaching a horse a new behaviour, it is essential that we make it as easy as possible for the horse to understand what we are asking of him. This is particularly important when teaching more complicated behaviours or movements, such as lateral work or high school movements. Breaking the behaviour down ensures that the horse can succeed at the task he is being asked to perform. Successful training will ensure the continued enjoyment of training by both horse and handler and this enjoyment will enhance the horse's trust in the handler. Two techniques which are particularly useful in breaking down training in a way which makes it easier for the horse to understand are shaping and chaining.

SHAPING

Shaping is defined as the reward of ever-closer approximations to a target behaviour, until that behaviour is achieved in full. For example, when you are first teaching a young horse to pick up his feet for them to be picked out, at first you only ask the horse to hold his leg a few centimetres off the ground for a couple of seconds in order to gain a reward. Over the course of training, he will be expected to hold his leg higher and for longer to receive the reward. These are closer and closer approximations to the final behaviour, which would be for the young horse to hold his hooves up calmly for as long as the handler desires.

CHAINING

Chaining is the combining of several different behaviours into a complete goal behaviour. Chaining is usually taught by forming the last part of the chain first and then working backwards through the chain, adding on the behaviours which go before until the start behaviour is finally added to the chain. This allows that as you add the chain backwards, the animal can do the new behaviour and then the rest of the known chain which is predictably rewarded. As the horse knows that performance of the rest of the chain will be rewarded, he will work for the opportunity to perform the rest of the chain. It is possible to chain forwards by reward and repetition of each part of the chain but this form of chaining is not as effective.

APPLYING SHAPING

Define the Target Behaviour

First, it is important to define exactly what the desired goal behaviour is; this prevents any ambiguity during training. The behaviour you want hasn't occurred or isn't reliable yet; it is the goal at the end of the shaping programme. Thus, in order to develop a successful behaviour-shaping programme it must be decided what the goal behaviour is to be.

Reinforce Successively Closer Approximations of the Target Behaviour

Make sure that you don't ask the horse to make too large a step in the training. Ensure that every task you teach is broken down into easily manageable steps. The goal behaviour is shaped and eventually reached by rewarding each step that is a nearer approximation of the goal behaviour. The further you can break a behaviour down, the easier it will be for the horse to understand, and the goal behaviour will be reached much more quickly than if the handler skips steps in the training. Small beginnings can build into big successes with the right nurturing.

The goal behaviour is shaped and eventually reached by reinforcing successively nearer approximations to that behaviour. The horse should be rewarded if he attempts to perform the behaviour or the shaping step desired by the handler. This reward will give the horse the confidence that he is on the right track and keep the training enjoyable for the horse. Each step which is closer to the desired goal behaviour should be rewarded, either through positive reinforcement or a clicker training structure. This is the concept of 'rewarding the try', which is often talked about by modern horse trainers.

If the horse becomes stuck at a particular step, it may be useful to go over the steps before, or break the step that the horse is stuck on down into smaller steps which will be easier for him to achieve. The horse must never be punished for not achieving a step; rather, it should be evaluated why the horse cannot achieve it. Reinforcing achievable and ever closer approximations will encourage confidence and learning in the horse. Shaping progresses more rapidly when the increases in the requirements for reinforcement are small. Shaping a behaviour is a balancing act between moving forward, so that the horse doesn't become fixed on any step, and establishing each step to ensure that the horse understands the step.

If the horse does a particularly good example of the shaping step or tries particularly hard, he may be given a jackpot reward which is larger or more valued by the horse (e.g. his favourite treat). This larger reward encourages the same quality of behaviour to reoccur.

Training Task: Shaping

Shaping the Leg Yield

The idea of this book is not to show the handler exactly how to train every movement and behaviour they will need from the horse. Its purpose is to merely give the handler the tools they will need to succeed at horse training in whichever area they choose, whether it be happy hacking, trick-training, dressage, eventing and so on. The examples below are given simply to show how shaping can be used to train a behaviour (in this case a leg yield) in a number of different contexts from ground training to ridden training.

Leg Yield From the Ground

The leg yield is the crossing of hind and front limbs, moving the horse in a sideways motion, whilst the horse is flexed in the opposite direction to the direction of movement.

Firstly, from the ground, get the horse to walk in front of you, with you standing just behind the shoulder. Hold the inside rein close to the horse's mouth and the outside rein in the other hand, just behind the horse's girth area; a stick can be held in this hand also. Ask the horse to walk with a light pressure of the hand on the girth area. Reward the horse as he walks forward. Establish the walk first. This behaviour can be shaped if the horse doesn't understand what is being asked of him. Remember to reward the horse when he begins to understand the concept of walking forwards in front of the handler. This is an example of breaking down behaviours for the horse to understand.

Once the horse is walking actively around the schooling area, ensure that he is flexed toward the handler by feeling the inside rein. The horse can then be asked to leg yield by moving the girth hand back a couple of inches (where the leg should be placed for a ridden leg yield) and applying a light pressure in time with the swing of the horse's barrel. As the horse's barrel swings away the pressure should be applied to encourage the horse to move further in the away direction. At the application of the pressure, the horse should yield slightly away from the handler (Fig. 11.1) Reward even the smallest yield, even if the horse's legs do not cross. Repeat the exercise, rewarding the yield. As the horse begins to understand the yield response, he should start to move in a more definitely sideways manner. Reward any effort by the horse to move sideways, especially if the horse crosses his limbs.

Once the horse has established that the pressure behind the girth means to yield sideways, you can shape the movement into the perfect leg yield by ensuring the horse moves evenly with his hind and front limbs, and rewarding a more and more precise behaviour. This is done by balancing the action of the reins and hand. If the outside rein is too loose, the horse will advance his shoulder too quickly and leave his quarters behind. If the hand is used in a hard manner, the horse will bend away from the hand rather than being straight. Remember, the hand is only a cue for the behaviour so never try to physically push the horse over.

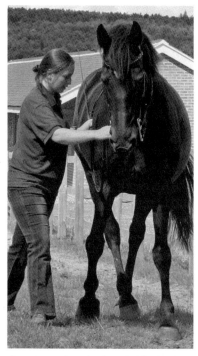

Figure 11.1   Jet demonstrating the leg yield.

Leg Yield on the Long Lines and Under Saddle

Leg yield on the long lines is shaped in exactly the same manner as a ground leg yield, except that the pressure of the hand a couple of inches behind the girth is replaced by the gentle touch of a cue stick (which can be a normal schooling whip). Similarly, a ridden leg yield is shaped in the same manner as a ground leg yield, except that the pressure of the hand/cue stick a couple of inches behind the girth is replaced by the leg.

Do Horses Dislike the Criteria for Reward Being Changed During Shaping?

I am sometimes asked whether horses will be disappointed or resentful of the criteria for reward being changed during shaping. An example is often given that if a child was rewarded for getting a

C grade at school but is capable of much more, the parents of the child would want to shape his behaviour towards achieving higher grades. If one day the child came home with a B grade, this grade would now be rewarded as it is a closer approximation to high grade achievement. Would the rewarding of the high grade cause resentment in the child as the criteria for reward have changed? Or would the child feel disappointment that C grades are no longer being rewarded and become demotivated?

This is where good timing and accuracy in training are needed. Ideally, when closer approximations to the desired behaviour begin to occur (such as a bigger cross during leg yielding) they will be rewarded with a more palatable or larger reward, but if the horse were to perform a less desirable approximation of the behaviour after the closer approximation (such as a small leg yield cross after the larger one), this would be rewarded with a smaller or less palatable reward. This way the reward is graduated with the closeness of the behaviour to the final desired goal. This ensures two things in training: first, that the horse is motivated to achieve the closer approximations as they carry higher reward values, and second that the horse can earn enough rewards to stay motivated to work during training. Once the horse has achieved the final behaviour and can perform it with ease on cue, the reward value can be lowered and the horse put on a variable schedule of reward. The behaviour is now established as a reward-predicting behaviour and will have a rewarding value to the horse so it is not necessary to continue with very high rewards to motivate the horse. Furthermore, the behaviour once taught will not require the horse to work so hard to understand and perform the behaviour and thus will not require the motivation of large rewards.

In the example of the child, this would mean that possibly the B grade could be rewarded with a trip out somewhere nice to encourage him to achieve the B grade again. However, if he came home with a C in the future he would be given a smaller reward. This would make sure that small efforts by the child were still rewarded but that he was motivated to try and achieve the higher grades. Once the child is regularly achieving a B grade the rewards would be slowly lowered, with occasional large rewards for very big efforts or A grades. This shaping could be continued until the child had reached the limits of his abilities.

Tips for Successful Shaping

We all Make Mistakes

During shaping you will have to make judgements about when to progress to the next shaping step; occasionally, you will be wrong. However, try not to worry but simply go back to the steps before. If you err on the side of caution, reinforcing behaviour at a given step more often than is necessary and making very small increases in the requirements for reinforcement, the worst that is likely to happen is that progress will be slow. If you make the mistake of moving too quickly, then progress will stop and you may see some strong emotional reactions from the horse as he becomes frustrated. Never punish the horse for being confused; failure to succeed at any step must only ever be ignored! Otherwise the horse will simply associate being confused with being punished and will become either fearful or aggressive the next time he feels confused. If progress breaks down, you can simply move back to a previous step of the shaping at which the horse can easily succeed, rewarding the horse for achieving this step and working forwards again. It's not the end of the world.

Writing It Down

One way you can gauge how successful you are being at shaping the desired behaviour is by noting what changes in behaviour are occurring. You can do this by writing down a plan of the steps you will take to reach the goal behaviour and subsequently ticking them off with the date of achievement. This way you can see the progress you and your horse are making even on the bad days. If you feel the shaping isn't progressing as you would like, the shaping plan can be re-evaluated – it is not set in stone.

For example, if you're training the horse to play football using clicker training, your shaping plan may look like Fig. 11.2.

The length and structure of the shaping plan will depend on the individual horse, how interested he is in the task, and his learning ability/style.

If your horse becomes stuck at a particular step, it may be useful to go over the steps before, or break down the step the horse is stuck on into smaller steps which will be easier for him to achieve. The horse must never be punished for not achieving a step; rather, it should be

Step	Target	Tick/Date
1	Horse walks towards ball on the ground – click/reward	
2	Horse accidentally touches ball with his hoof – click/reward	
3	Horse deliberately touches ball with hoof – click/reward	
4	Horse touches ball with hoof and it moves – click/reward	
5	Horse touches ball with hoof, causing it to move, and follows it – click/reward	
6	Horse plays football – click/reward	
7	Goal = horse playing football	

Figure 11.2   Shaping plan for teaching the horse to play football.

evaluated why he cannot achieve it. Reinforcing achievable and ever closer approximations will encourage confidence and learning in your horse. Shaping progresses more rapidly when the steps are smaller and more achievable than if they are fewer and large.

How Long Should a Behaviour Take to Shape?

Every horse is an individual and will require the programme to progress at a particular pace. The length of time will depend on the horse's motivation, physical ability to perform the behaviour, how natural the behaviour is to the horse, the skill of the trainer and the learning ability of the horse. There is no correct timetable for training a behaviour, only the timetable that is correct for your individual horse.

If you try to adhere to a strict timetable, you are likely to become frustrated if the horse requires more time to learn the behaviour than you have allowed. Always wait until the horse is ready to move on to the next step before progressing. Often, by going at the horse's pace you will reach the goal behaviour quicker than if you become obsessed by the end result and try and move too quickly. Confusing the horse by moving too quickly will only result in the training having to go back a couple of stages and thus taking longer. To progress quickly, you must be correct and considered in your training. Take time and pride in your training, and enjoy the process of training, as well as the end result. Reward yourself and the horse for every new step completed.

Training Task: More Complicated Shaping – Teaching the Spanish Walk

The Spanish walk is a fun exercise to teach the horse, as well as being a fantastic exercise for strengthening the lifting and extensor muscles of the horse's shoulders. Large improvements in the horse's movement can often be seen as he becomes stronger in his shoulders.

Step 1 – Picking Up the Leg

Teach the horse to pick up his leg to a light touch of the stick. You should never hit the horse's legs with the stick, only the lightest touch should be used. Use clicker training or positive reinforcement to reward even the smallest lift at first. This stage should be repeated until the horse lifts both legs reliably to a very light touch, or even simply a movement of the cue stick (Fig. 11.3).

Figure 11.3   Billy demonstrating step 1.

Step 2 – Asking for the Extension of the Foreleg

To achieve the extension necessary for Spanish walk, teach the horse to target the cue stick with his foreleg. This targeting behaviour using the foreleg can be induced by gently touching the horse's leg with the stick when he brings it forwards slightly and then immediately rewarding the touch. The horse will realise that he should aim to touch the stick. Then, gently ask for more extension from the horse by placing the stick further away and higher. Never stretch the horse beyond the point where he is comfortable. Short periods of Spanish walk practice are much more productive for strengthening the shoulders of the horse and the extensor muscle than long periods. The horse should never be tired at the end of a session. By not using force during training, the horse will often let you know when he is tired. The end result of extension training should be the jambette, which looks like a salute. The horse should be strong enough to hold the jambette for at least a couple of seconds. The height of the jambette will depend on the conformation and flexibility of the horse (Fig. 11.4).

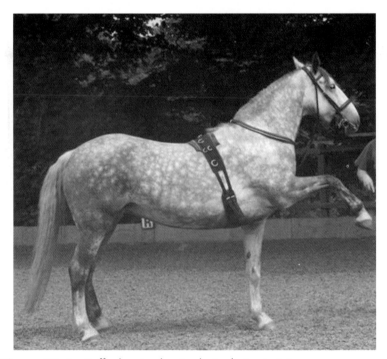

Figure 11.4   Saffy showing her jambette during training.

Step 3 – Lifting and Walking

Once the horse can hold a jambette comfortably for a couple of seconds and seems to find the exercise relatively easy, the training can progress to asking him to lift and move. Simply have the horse walking beside you and then occasionally ask him to jambette with one leg in time with the walk. The leg furthest from the handler is often the best to ask for. Repeat this on both sides of the horse until he is balanced and strong enough to do step–jambette–step on both sides with one leg. Once this movement is established, then ask him to lift each leg in turn in time with the walk. Again, remember to reward every effort the horse makes to try and perform the behaviour desired. The reward will show the horse that he was correct and give him motivation to continue to try for the handler. Simply repeat the exercise until the horse can easily lift each foreleg alternately in time with the walk (Fig. 11.5).

These are the basic steps of teaching the Spanish walk. However, other steps may need to be added or removed dependent on the horse. For example, some horses (although this is rare) will offer alternate foreleg lifts from the beginning of training, but for others steps may need to be added for the horse to understand the concept of the Spanish walk.

Figure 11.5   Saffy learning the Spanish walk.

Your Imagination Is the Only Limit

Every behaviour can be broken down so that it is easy for the horse to understand. The imagination of the trainer and the physical ability of the horse are the only things that will limit what you can achieve. If you get stuck with training, writing down what you want to achieve, and how you intend to achieve it, can often lift trainer's block. This can also work if you get stuck training a move that the horse doesn't seem to understand. Every behaviour ever required from the horse can be broken down in a way that makes it easy for the horse to succeed, from simple behaviours such as transitions to much harder ones such as flying changes or high school moves such as the lavade. Once a horse has learned a behaviour through shaping, he can be put onto a variable schedule of reinforcement as explained in Chapter 6.

Common Mistakes in Behaviour Shaping

Bad Timing

Bad timing of reward will often inadvertently cause the trainer to reinforce a behaviour which is not required or wanted. If this happens the horse will try and perform the unwanted behaviour in the future; should this happen, simply ignore the unwanted behaviour and accurately reward the desired behaviour when it next occurs. Never punish the horse for performing the unwanted behaviour, as at this point the horse will believe that it is the behaviour the handler desires. Punishing this behaviour, when its occurrence is the fault of the handler, would be highly unfair to the horse and only further hamper training, as well as breaking the trust of the horse in the handler.

Failing to Reinforce

If the horse achieves a step toward the goal behaviour and the handler fails to reward him, he is less likely to perform the behaviour again, since the previous step was rewarded but the advancement wasn't. The horse may therefore become stuck on a step of the shaping. To be a good trainer, it is necessary to reward the horse for even the smallest improvement in performance.

Asking Too Much

As humans we tend to think only about the end result of the training. However, the horse has no idea what the intended end result is. It is therefore necessary, as a trainer, to view the training from the horse's point of view and to make the process of training both enjoyable and understandable for the horse, rather than the human's desired end result being the entire point of the training. If you ask too much you will get very little, or even nothing, from the horse.

APPLYING CHAINING

Another technique that can be useful to teach the horse desired behaviours is chaining. Chaining is simply the linking of behaviours in a sequence so that they become a more complex behaviour. Each behaviour leads to another, in a sequence.

The secrets to chaining are:

- making sure that the behaviours are taught with the last behaviours chained first so that the end of the chain is predictable in sequence and reward
- building the chain in steps so that it is easy for the horse to understand
- reinforcing the chain of behaviours at the end of the chain.

The behaviour is built up from component behaviours already known by the horse, which are linked together. Let's say that you have behaviours A, B and C that you want to link together to from the behaviour 'ABC'. The chain would be built up like this.

Cue behaviour C and reward. Then cue behaviour B and then C and reward. Once established so that asking for behaviour B automatically cues the performance of C, add behaviour A onto the beginning of the sequence. The performance of behaviour A gives the horse the chance to be cued for the rest of the chain and receive the predicted reward. Finally after repetition, the cueing of behaviour A will trigger the entire chain as the horse knows that the final behaviour is the rewarded one.

A useful example of chaining during training is gate opening and closing whilst hacking. Gate opening is a task most of us will have tackled at some point in our lives with our horse and it is useful to be able to open and close the gate whilst remaining mounted. Gate opening requires the horse to be able to do three things: be steered by the rider holding the reins in one hand (the other hand will be holding the gate), yield their hindquarters over, and finally back up. These three abilities should be established using one of the techniques described in the book, before attempting to train the horse to open and close gates. To open a gate, the horse has to chain these individual behaviours together to perform the task. With a gate that opens towards the horse, the horse will need to chain the behaviours in the following way: first, the rider will need to steer the horse into position next to the gate and hold the gate in one hand and the horse in the other; the horse will then have to rein back to open the gate towards him; once the gate is open, the rider is required to hold the gate whilst the horse yields around the gate, so that they are on the other side of the gate; and finally the horse will need to rein back again to close the gate. During training the necessary behaviours should be chained together in sequence, starting by teaching the last behaviour (the rein back to close the gate) with an assistant helping with gate control. So first the horse learns to rein back to close the gate for reward. Then he learns to yield round the gate and shut it for reward and finally to open the gate through reining back for the chance to yield around the gate and rein back to close it and receive the predicted reward. The horse will soon be able to predict the behavioural sequence and, after practice, be able to perform the gate opening and closing task easily.

Chaining Forwards

Chaining forwards is also possible although not as effective as chaining backwards as the process relies only on repetition rather than repetition and the motivation of a predictable reward.

Cue behaviour A → cue behaviour B immediately following A → reward and repeat until behaviour A automatically cues behaviour B. Repeat A → B → cue behaviour C → reward and repeat until behaviour A automatically cues behaviours B and C. Repetition and reward of the sequence will ensure that the component behaviours A, B and C combine to form the behaviour 'ABC' on the cue of behaviour A.

A good example of chaining is to teach the horse to fetch. Fetch consists of three component behaviours:

1. Going to the object to be fetched, which can be cued by saying 'go' or pointing to the object. This can be taught by extending the targeting exercise to distance targeting objects.
2. Picking up the object to be fetched. This behaviour can be really easy for horses who naturally like to mouth things, but difficult for those who don't want to pick up objects in their mouth. This behaviour may require some shaping in itself to ensure the horse is happy to hold the object in his mouth for a period of time. Simply reward the horse for holding the object for progressively longer periods of time.
3. The horse returning to the handler with the fetched object. This behaviour can be cued with the 'come'. At first, only expect the horse to go a tiny distance towards the handler and increase the distance once the horse understands to come to the handler with the object.

This sequence is to be built up as follows:

- Cue 1 → reward and repeat until the horse reliably distance targets the object.
- Cue 1 → cue 2 → reward and repeat until the horse picks up the object of his own accord without the 2 cue and thus has chained behaviours 1 and 2.
- Cue 1 → 2 → cue 3 → again reward and repeat until the horse picks up the object of his own accord and returns to the owner without the 2 or 3 behaviours cue and thus has chained behaviours 1, 2 and 3 and the fetch behaviour is established.

The fetch can also be chained backwards by teaching the horse to pick up and give the object first and then teaching him to go to the object (Fig. 11.6).

If the horse gets stuck during training, he can be supported with cues for the next behaviours and rewards for trying.

The common mistakes made in the training of chaining are almost identical to those made during shaping; bad timing of reward causing the wrong behaviour to be reinforced, failure to reward an advancement in the chaining of the steps so that the horse becomes stuck on a step, or asking too much of the horse before he is ready.

Figure 11.6   AJ demonstrating the fetch.

CONCLUSION

Shaping and chaining are important concepts to master, so that you and your horse may succeed in even the complex training tasks that you may encounter during your life together. As you can see by the examples explained in this chapter, it may be necessary to break down a task into smaller, more understandable steps for the horse, whether you want to hack or event. During your training, if you find that the horse is not understanding what is required of him, see if the task can be broken down into smaller step. Often, the less you ask of your horse in one go, the faster he will progress and the more relaxed and attentive he will be during training.

LEARNING RECAP

Reiterating the key points of the chapter and the most important concepts to understand to make your training as successful as possible.

Key Terms	Recap of Definition and Important Concepts
Shaping	Shaping is defined as the reward of ever-closer approximations to a target behaviour, until that behaviour is achieved in full.
Chaining	Chaining is the combining of several different behaviours into a complete goal behaviour. The behaviours should be gradually linked together in sequence until the horse can predict every step in the chain and perform the entire task.

MY TRAINING LOG – STEP BY STEP

You can use this table to help you break down a behaviour that you wish to train into smaller parts for shaping or chaining. This can be used for anything from training simple commands to very complex ones. Not all the steps have to be used for every behaviour.

Step	Description of Step	Notes	Date Achieved
1			
2			
3			
4			
5			
6			
7			
8			
9			
10			
11			
12			

13			
14			
15			
16			
17			
18			
19			

Goal Behaviour ....

Knowing Your Horse: A Guide to Equine Learning, Training and Behaviour
Emma Lethbridge
9781405191647

Overcoming Fears and Phobias

One of the biggest challenges of horse ownership and training is overcoming any fears or phobias that the horse may have. Horses are capable of feeling fear in a similar way to humans. Fear is a response to any stimulus that the horse believes will threaten his future survival or well-being, regardless of the likelihood of the stimulus hurting the horse, as they are not rational creatures when afraid. If the fear prevents the horse from functioning in his environment it can be termed a phobia. For example, if the horse is so afraid of the feed bucket that he won't eat, and so loses weight, then the horse has a phobia about his feed bucket.

Fears may be expressed by horses in several different ways, the most common being flight, fight, freeze or faint. Most horse owners will have experienced 'flight' from a scared horse in the form of a spook or bolt behaviour. However, if cornered or provoked, the horse may also become aggressive, 'fight', stand rigidly, 'freeze' or fall to the ground, 'faint'. It is important to train the horse in a way that minimises his fears, to ensure the safety of both the horse and his handlers, as well as the psychological well-being of the horse.

PREVENTION IS BETTER THAN CURE

Ideally the horse's training starts in his first year of life, when he is still reasonably neophilic (curious about new objects and experiences, rather than fearful). Although there are no official data about the length of this period, certainly training should start within the horse's first year of life, in order for him to ultimately be well adjusted to live a contented life with humans. The horse should be introduced to the majority of experiences he will encounter during his life, i.e. horse boxes, trailers, clippers, farriers, hose pipes and interacting with other humans and horses, whilst he is young. The introduction of the young horse to all stimuli and events he is likely to encounter in his life so that he is comfortable around these stimuli is known as 'habituation'. The process of introducing the horse to his social peers and teaching him how to interact with his peers in different situations is known as 'socialisation'. Habituation and socialisation should be approached in a way that creates pleasant, fear-free memories of these events. As long as the horse is introduced to the stimuli in a positive, prepared and gradual manner, both habituation and socialisation should be easy and enjoyable. This preparation ensures the horse is comfortable with the majority of life experiences he is likely to encounter from a young age. Introducing horses to lots of unusual experiences whilst they are young also allows them to learn how to respond to new and unusual experiences without panicking (Figs 12.1, 12.2).

Figure 12.1   Ittingston Blackthorn being introduced to the trailer at two months old.

Figure 12.2   Two-year-old Love Me Tender being introduced to plastic by her owner Rachel.

Imprint Training Versus Training the Older Foal

There is a recent theory in horse training based on the biological process of imprinting. The theory postulates that an intense period of handling when the foal is neonatal (just born) will create a horse that is less reactive and more accepting of human contact and situations he is likely to encounter in his life, such as shoeing and medical procedures. However, research on foal handling is undecided on whether such handling is successful and whether the stress it puts on the foal and dam is justified and won't produce problems by interfering with the bonding between the foal and mare.

Simpson (2002) studied 15 foals, seven of which were handled extensively as neonates and eight of which were not handled. The foals were handled from two to eight hours after birth, introducing a series of stimuli and experiences, such as handling the foal's feet and nose. This procedure was repeated until the foal no longer resisted or reacted negatively and continued daily for a total of five days. The foals were tested for reactivity and amiability at four months of age. The study found that there was a general reduction in reactivity and stress in the neonatally handled foals in comparison to the other foals. However, there was no difference in reactivity to specific stimuli such as feet tapping and nose handling.

Many other studies have found that this neonatal handling is not effective at creating easily handleable horses. Williams *et al.* (2002) found that neonatal training had no effect on the behaviour of foals after three months of age. By three months of age the neonatally handled foals were of similar reactivity to the control foals in the study and showed no significant difference in their reactions to any stimuli. A further study by Williams *et al.* (2003) investigated 131 foals that were separated into groups and were trained with either no imprint training, imprint training at 0, 12, 24 and 48 hours after birth, or imprint training at one of 0, 12, 24, 48 or 72 hours after birth. The foals were then left unhandled until six months of age when they were tested for manageability. There was no significant overall difference between the foals' manageability regardless of any neonatal handling procedure, so the neonatal training was therefore concluded to be ineffective.

In addition, a study by Lansade *et al.* (2004) found that any difference in manageability correlated with neonatal handling may only be short term. These authors studied 26 Welsh foals, 13 of which were handled from birth daily for 14 days and 13 were not handled and used as control comparisons. The neonatal handling procedure included putting on the halter, touching all parts of the foal's body, picking up the foal's feet and leading. The foals were tested for reactivity and manageability two days, three months, six months and one year after the final neonatal handling procedure. The results showed that neonatal handling had only short-term effects on the foals' behaviour during handling sessions and that by six months, the neonatally handled foals were only easier to handle during one of the tests and that by one year there was no difference in the behaviour of the foals.

The natural conclusion to draw from the above studies is that the possible, short-term benefits of neonatal handling do not justify the potential stress caused to the new foal and its dam, and the possible interruption of bonding and feeding behaviours that may be caused by such early handling. This is not to say that gradual non-intensive training of the older foals can not be highly beneficial. For example, Lansade *et al.* (2003) found that training foals at and around weaning can have highly beneficial effects that could last for up to 18 months, and that weaning may thus be an ideal time to introduce the foal to training.

OVERCOMING ESTABLISHED FEARS AND PHOBIAS

There may be times when, despite an owner or trainer's best efforts, a young horse may have a bad experience resulting in fear. Alternatively, the young horse may innately develop a fear of acertain experience or object due to his nature or a lack of habituation or socialisation with that stimulus. Also, many owners do not own their horses from such a young age and the horse may come to the owner with fears of certain objects or experiences already established. Many people confuse fear with stubbornness. Horses are rarely if ever 'stubborn', but they do act in a way that they perceive will best ensure their survival. This may include trying not to leave the yard which they know is safe, not going into the 'horse-eating' trailer or approaching the whirling blades humans call clippers. If the horse is reluctant to approach a situation, for example hacking or being clipped, or to approach an object during training, it is likely that he is fearful of the object or situation and must be trained in a gentle, gradual and sympathetic way to overcome this fear. Sympathetic training acknowledges that the horse is being fearful and not 'stubborn' or 'naughty' and works to help the horse overcome the fear.

It is possible for a horse to unlearn these fear responses with patience and correct training. There are several methods that can be used to help a horse overcome his fears. These include:

- habituation
- flooding
- systematic desensitisation
- counter conditioning.

HABITUATION

Habituation is the diminishing of a behavioural and/or biological response (i.e. fear) to a certain stimulus, i.e. an object or situation, due to repeated exposure to that stimulus. An example of biological habituation in humans is the apparent loss of its flavour when gum is chewed for a while; the gum doesn't actually lose its flavour, the body just stops responding to the taste. Habituation to a fearful stimulus works in a similar manner – the body just gets used to the presence of the stimulus and ceases to respond in a fearful manner.

This response is necessary for the horse to be well adapted to his environment. The repetition of exposure to the stimulus, as long as it is neither overtly threatening to the horse nor pleasurable, will cause the horse to stop responding to the presence of the stimulus.

For example, if a horse is fearful of bicycles, then a repeated reasonably neutral experience of a bicycle can diminish a fear response as the horse learns that he comes to no harm in the company of bicycles.

For habituation of a fear response to be successful, the stimulus must not be presented in a way which causes the horse to panic. The meeting of the horse with the stimulus must be as emotionally neutral as possible so that the horse comes to discover that the stimulus is not harmful.

Very occasionally, a horse may be encountered who does not respond to the stimulus through habituation, but becomes more fearful of the stimulus through repeated exposure. Although these horses are very rare it may be that habituation is not the correct technique to use for these animals.

If the horse is not habituating to the stimulus, it is also worth considering that the following factors may be preventing habituation from occurring:

- If the horse is intensely fearful of the stimulus, his own fear may sustain the behavioural response and cause him to perceive the stimulus as harmful, preventing habituation to the stimulus.
- If the horse's reactions cause the stimulus to be removed from his environment, e.g. if the horse bolts, then he may believe that those reactions allowed him to escape from the stimulus. The horse will be conditioned through negative reinforcement (the reinforcement of a behaviour through escaping an undesirable stimulus) to bolt from the fearful stimulus whenever it is presented. During the presentation of the stimulus, the horse must not be made to act in a way which he could construe as having allowed him to escape the stimulus.

FLOODING

During flooding the fearful stimulus is presented to the horse in an area from which he cannot escape. The horse will experience the fear reaction to the stimulus, but should eventually calm down as the fear response diminishes. The horse is not allowed to move from the fearful stimulus until the fear response has ceased. The horse's body cannot maintain the fear reaction forever and so the horse must calm to the presence of the stimulus over time and come to realise that it is not fearful.

Flooding is a controversial way of dealing with phobias and for safety reasons I would not recommend its use during training. During flooding, the horse is put under immense stress, especially if he is phobic of the fearful stimulus. It is also questionable whether it is ethical to place the horse under so much stress, especially as there are more sympathetic and effective approaches which don't put the horse in a position of such extreme fear. Many would certainly consider it against the horse's physical and psychological welfare to use flooding during training.

Furthermore, when using flooding, the horse is put in a position where panic is likely. This can have two undesirable consequences. First, if the horse panics, it could result in potential injury to the horse, to surrounding property and to any handlers near the horse at the time. A panicking horse is a very dangerous thing. Second, if the horse manages to escape the fearful stimulus by panicking or by using his strength against a human before the fear response has ceased, he may learn to panic or use his strength in order to escape fearful stimuli. This would be extremely dangerous for future handlers of the horse. For example, many horses are afraid of clippers. If the horse is forced to face clippers in a situation where he cannot choose to move away, then he may panic and try to escape. Should the horse achieve this escape by running over the handler, he will have learnt that to escape the scary stimulus (the clippers) he must run over his handler. In the future, if the horse encounters the clippers (or possibly other fear-inducing stimuli), his immediate reaction will be to try and escape the stimulus in the same way as before – by running over the handler. The horse will have been conditioned through negative reinforcement to run over the handler, an extremely dangerous learned response.

SYSTEMATIC DESENSITISATION

Systematic desensitisation is a more sympathetic and generally safer way to train a horse to overcome his fears. A gradual desensitisation to a fearful stimulus can be achieved through gradual, systematic introduction to that stimulus, so that the horse learns to control his reaction to the stimulus, without being overfaced by it.

During systematic desensitisation the horse is gradually introduced to the stimulus he finds fearful, at a level he can cope with. Once the horse is happy with this level of stimulus exposure, the stimulus can be presented to the horse in a manner that is a little more intense but with which the horse can still cope without panicking. Again, once the horse is happy and calm with this level of exposure, the presentation of the stimulus can be increased again until the horse is eventually calm during any intensity of exposure.

The main advantage of systematic desensitisation is that it minimises the chance of the horse panicking and hurting either himself or others. However, this technique does require the handler to read the horse well, so that the stimulus is presented at a level that is correct for the horse and does not cause panic. It is important to also remember that we all make mistakes; if the horse starts to panic, simply re-present the stimulus at the lower level of exposure that the horse was happy with and work up to a more intense exposure slowly, giving the horse enough time to desensitise to the stimulus at each level of intensity.

It is important to allow the horse to dictate the rate of desensitisation. Pushing a time frame onto the training is only a quick way to failure. Take your time and listen to the horse. Every horse is an individual and differs both in his innate personality and in his life experiences. The speed of each horse's desensitisation to a stimulus will reflect this fact. The rate of desensitisation will also depend on how fearful the horse is of the stimulus and his experience of the stimulus in the past, e.g. a horse that is scared of a horse box because it is a small, dark space will respond differently through the desensitisation than a horse who is fearful of the horse box because of a traffic accident experienced whilst in a horse box.

Introducing fearful stimuli in a sympathetic and gradual way will not only help the horse to overcome his fear, but will also teach him to control his responses and to react in a controlled and safe manner.

COUNTER CONDITIONING

As described previously, counter conditioning is the conditioning of a desired response that is incompatible with the undesired one, so that only the desired reaction occurs. For example, if a horse is fearful of hose pipes, you would reward him for any calm behaviour around hose pipes. As the horse cannot be fearful and calm at the same time and calm behaviour is now more rewarding, the horse will start to perform calm behaviour instead of fearful behaviour in response to the hose pipe. Counter conditioning can be used to help the horse to overcome any of his fears. A calm response is rewarded and conditioned to replace a fearful one in the case of fears and phobias.

Counter conditioning can be achieved using positive reinforcement or clicker training. The horse is rewarded whilst calm in the presence of the fearful stimulus. This reward causes the horse to eventually see the presence of the fearful stimulus as a desirable occurrence, rather than a fearful one, and conditions the horse to react calmly when exposed to previously scary stimuli.

The application of counter conditioning is particularly useful if the fearful stimulus is one that the horse has to encounter on a regular basis in his routine, training or health checks, i.e. the farrier or dentist. If the horse can learn to enjoy these experiences he will be far more content in his life with humans.

COMBINING SYSTEMATIC DESENSITISATION AND COUNTER CONDITIONING

Systematic desensitisation and counter conditioning can be combined during training to great effect. The gradual introduction of the stimulus at a rate the horse can cope with without inducing panic, combined with the rewarding of good calm behaviour in the presence of the stimulus, can encourage the horse to not only be happy with the presence of the stimulus, but see it as a desirable occurrence. The training of the horse to overcome his fears is also likely to occur with maximum efficiency due to the beneficial elements of both techniques, while minimising the chance of the horse panicking. This form of remedial training makes the process of helping the horse overcome his fears as pleasurable and safe for horse and handler as possible.

Which Method of Fear-Conquering Training Is Most Effective?

Habituation, systematic desensitisation and counter conditioning have been compared with regard to their effectiveness in diminishing a fear response in horses by Christensen *et al.* (2006). The fearful stimulus the horses were exposed to was a white nylon bag. It was found through the study that the most effective method of training to help the horse overcome his fear was systematic desensitisation; these horses overcame their fear fastest and every one of the horses managed to cease his flight response in reaction to the bag stimulus. The combination of systematic desensitisation and counter conditioning was not tested in the study.

An Example of Combining Counter Conditioning and Systematic Desensitisation

Here is the herd, demonstrating how different individual horses can be when it comes to their fears. Toby (the skewbald horse) is the only horse in the picture who is afraid of the purple inflatable, the others think it is a great toy (Fig. 12.3a).

Toby was gently encouraged to approach the inflatable through systematic desensitisation and rewarded for calm behaviour around it and especially when he was brave enough to approach it. After a

(a)

Figure 12.3a–c   Toby overcoming his fear of the purple inflatable via the use of systematic desensitisation and counter conditioning.

(b)   (c)

Figure 12.3a–c   (Cont'd)

time, Toby was confident enough to approach the inflatable on his own without the handler and even play with it (Fig. 12.3b, c).

Can Horses Generalise Habituation Training?

A study by Christensen *et al.* (2008a) investigated whether horses could generalise a habituation response to many objects by presenting the objects one after another during a young stallion's feed time. The six objects were a ball, barrel, board, box, cone and cylinder which were presented in sequence. The objects were of a similar size but different in colour. The horses received many two-minute exposures to the object. However, despite this habituation there was no decrease in fear reaction to a novel stimulus as the object number increased, in comparison to unhabituated horses. However, a supplementary experiment by the same team used objects of a similar size and colour. This study found that horses could generalise between very similar objects and that colour may be a key factor. The horses showed a significant reduction in fearful behaviour and heart rate as the number of objects increased. It is concluded that some generalisation of the habituation response might be very possible, but a high consistency of colour, size and shape between objects is required for generalisation to occur.

In training this means that if a horse is helped to overcome his fear of an object such as a plastic bag, he may be able to transfer this trained, calm response to other similar objects in their environment (such as different types of plastic bags) without any or only a small amount of further training.

Does Having a Calm Companion Horse Help a Nervous Horse Overcome His Fear?

It is often thought within the horse world that having a calm companion horse can reduce fear in young and/or nervous horses in fearful situations. For example, when young horses are first taken onto the roads it is often considered good practice to have an older, very experienced and calm horse go along as a companion and guide for the younger horse to help calm him should he become fearful. Although, as social animals, it would seem logical that horses would look to their peers for cues as to how to behave in a fearful situations, until recently there was no scientific evidence of such an effect in horses as it had not been studied.

However, a recent study by Christensen *et al.* (2008b) found evidence of a calming effect from non-fearful companion horses in novel fearful situations. These authors used 36 two-year-old stallions in the experiment. Half of the stallions were to be used as companions and half as test horses. The companion stallions were further split into two groups: half were conditioned to be reliably calm around a test stimulus through habituation. The other half were not habituated to the test stimulus and were fearful of it. Christensen *et al.* found that test horses who were paired with calm companions showed significantly fewer fear reactions and lower heart rates (a measure of fear) than horses paired with unhabituated, fearful companion horses. It was also found that when the companion horses were taken away, those horses that had been paired with calm companions remained less fearful of the test stimulus than horses that had been paired with fearful companions. It was concluded from the study that interaction with a calm companion horse during training can help young and nervous horses to overcome their fears.

LEARNING RECAP

Reiterating the key points of the chapter and the most important concepts to understand to make your training as successful as possible.

Key Terms	Recap of Definition and Important Concepts
Socialisation	Socialisation is the introducing of a young horse to all the situations he will need to be comfortable with for a contented life with his equine peers, whilst he is still open to new experiences.
Habituation	Habituation is the diminishing of a behavioural and/or biological response (i.e. fear) to a certain stimulus, i.e. an object or situation, due to repeated exposure to that stimulus.
Flooding	Flooding consists of presenting the fearful stimulus to the horse in an area from which the horse cannot escape. The horse will experience an elevated fear reaction to the stimulus, but should eventually calm down as the fear response diminishes. However, this method is not recommended in training, as there are associated dangers that should be noted and have been explained in the chapter.
Systematic desensitisation	A gradual desensitisation to a fearful stimulus can be achieved through gradual, systematic introduction to that stimulus, so that the horse learns to control his reaction to the stimulus without being overfaced by it.
Counter conditioning	Counter conditioning is the conditioning of an incompatible response to the undesired one, so that only the desired reaction occurs.

Case Studies: Helping Horses Overcome Their Fears

Rolo's Story

Rolo's owner Allie explains – 'During the winter Rolo pulled muscles in his back. I noticed this when I tried to put his tack on one day. The bridle went on without a problem but he began to fidget when I put the saddle on. Not realising what had happened I mounted him – he immediately bucked and threw me off. This is something he had never done before! Straight away I had his back checked and the problem was identified and rectified over the course of a couple of months. Eventually it was time to tack him up again. This time though, I couldn't even get the bit in his mouth. He would clamp it shut then throw his head in the air and I couldn't even get near him with the saddle! This went on for a couple of weeks without improvement. It even became a struggle getting him in from the field. People suggested everything including calmers, but I didn't want to go down that route, as I know this isn't normal behaviour.

In the first session Emma introduced Rolo and me to the concept of clicker training. I had heard of clicker training with dogs, but not horses. He has always enjoyed his food and it worked. By the end of that session I could fully tack him up! By the time I saw Emma again, putting his tack on wasn't an issue any more and he didn't run away in the field any longer. During the second session, we worked on mounting at the mounting block. I used to mount him from the ground, but since his injury I wanted to use a mounting block. At first he became very agitated and wouldn't stand next to it. By the end of the session he would walk up to it, stand still and wait until I'd mounted. Rolo and I have our great relationship back again.'

Solution

Rolo had developed a fear of the saddle, bridle and mounting block due to the memory of the pain that had occurred when his back was injured. The anxiety of being tacked and mounted remained, even once the pain had been relieved and he was fully healed.

First, we approached the saddling and bridling using counter conditioning (replacing a fearful response with a calm, still response to being tacked) through clicker training. We gradually asked Rolo to accept the bridle by shaping his behaviour. Refusal to stand still or comply is never punished, just not rewarded. In the beginning, if he allowed the bit near his mouth we clicked and rewarded him with an appropriate food reward, turning a previously unpleasant experience into a rewarding one. We gradually asked Rolo to open his mouth for the bit and then to allow the bridle to be completely put on. This slow introduction of the bit and bridle combines systematic desensitisation and counter conditioning. Using these techniques together can be very effective in helping horses to overcome their fears. We repeated this several times until Rolo was completely calm and even enjoying being bridled (Fig. 12.4).

This process was repeated with the saddle. Rolo was clicked and rewarded for being calm and still when the saddle was approaching. Once he was happy with the saddle approaching, we gradually shaped his behaviour further by asking him to remain calm while the saddle was being put on and girthed.

Figure 12.4   Rolo overcoming his fear of tack and the mounting block.

Again, the saddle was introduced slowly, so that Rolo was systematically desensitised to the saddle and was not overfaced during any point in the training. Rolo was clicked and rewarded if he made an attempt to stand still and be calm. Once Rolo had learned that the saddle was not going to hurt him and that saddling was in fact a pleasant, rather than an unpleasant experience, he would stand calmly to be saddled.

In the next session, we asked Rolo to stand at the mounting block to be mounted. We proceeded by gradually introducing the mounting block and click-rewarding calm, still behaviour. As the mounting block is where Rolo's accident happened, it was particularly important to reintroduce the block at a pace with which Rolo was happy. At first we asked Rolo to simply stand quietly by the mounting block. Once he was calm and happy and would stand still reliably, we further shaped this behaviour by asking Rolo to stand in the same manner with Allie standing on the mounting block and then preparing to mount him. Finally, Rolo allowed Allie to mount him without moving or becoming agitated, and this was repeated and click-rewarded each time.

Allie was very dedicated to working with Rolo in this sympathetic and kind manner and therefore Rolo has regained his trust of being saddled, bridled and mounted quickly and continues to allow himself to be tacked and mounted without event.

Ptolomy's Fear of the Farrier

Ptolomy has anxiety about having his feet trimmed, probably caused by experiences in his past. This anxiety causes him to be unpredictable and, because of his impressive stature at over 17hh, dangerous during trimming. We decided that the best way to help Ptolomy overcome his anxiety when being trimmed would be to use a combination of counter conditioning and desensitisation to help him enjoy being trimmed, by associating trimming with rewards and pleasure, rather than with fear.

We started by introducing Ptolomy to clicker training by forming an association between the click and the receiving of a food treat. Once he understood that the click predicted the arrival of a food reward, we applied the clicker training to the trimming. At first, we only asked for Ptolomy to lift his feet calmly for the trimmer, Emily Smedley, to receive his click and reward. He quickly realised that only calm behaviour resulted in him getting a reward and that foot throwing, stamping and kicking out was ignored and received no such reward. Ptolomy was soon standing quietly whilst Emily held and handled his feet. If he tried to struggle and then relaxed without snatching his foot away from Emily, then he was rewarded once relaxed.

After Ptolomy was easily lifting and holding his feet calmly for Emily, we further shaped this new behavioural response by asking him to lift and hold his feet calmly whilst Emily ran a rasp around his feet. Once again, he quickly got the idea that standing calmly resulted in the receiving of a click and reward and soon Emily could lightly trim all of Ptolomy's feet both in hand and with the hoof stand and he would even offer his foot to be trimmed (Fig. 12.5).

Ptolomy was beginning to enjoy the process of trimming and was significantly less fearful of it. The whole session lasted less than an hour to ensure that Ptolomy was not overfaced.

Emma and Emily carried on Ptolomy's training and he continues to improve with each trim and now does not find being trimmed a fearful experience. As Ptolomy continues he will be put on a more variable schedule of reinforcement and be rewarded for longer periods of calmness during trimming.

Figure 12.5   Ptolomy now happy to be trimmed.

Calming Dylan, the Nervous Horse

Terri is Dylan's owner – 'In January 2004 we bought Dylan, a six-year-old Dutch Warmblood X Irish Sports Horse, with a view to general riding fun and maybe competing at local shows. He was at a show-jumping yard where he was competing at BSJA Novice level. On moving him to the rural farm stabling with only two other horses for company, he became unsettled and progressively became more jumpy and unreliable when ridden out, but remained calm and easy to handle within the stable environment. To avoid the situation getting dangerous, we decided to stop riding him out and return to basics. For the next four months or so we put in a lot of groundwork time, lunging, etc. and endeavouring to build mutual trust and respect. By January 2005, we were back riding and hacking out through the woods and started having weekly lessons. Gradually both Dylan and my confidence increased. His school work progressed, albeit slowly at times. He was argumentative and he was very easily distracted, especially by noises, often with explosive results. By January 2006, Dylan could be ridden out on his own (even when it was very windy) and his school work had become more collected, he worked more in self-carriage and we were generally happy with his slow but positive progress.

In April 2007 Dylan was unfortunately diagnosed with laminitis which resulted in two weeks strict box rest, followed by a further four weeks of box rest, but he was allowed to go out in hand for five minutes twice a day, increasing to 40 minutes. We all found this seriously stressful; even though he was sedated he became quite unpredictable and dangerous when the sedatives were wearing off and this also made walking out in hand very exciting. Although his physical recovery went according to plan, when I started to ride Dylan he had become quite spooky and after a few weeks got worse, to the point when he saw a friend's car coming towards us down the farm drive and span round in a total panic and headed home (totally out of character as before traffic was not a problem – he coped with tractors towing trailers loaded up with silage bales with flashing lights down single track lanes, etc.). Thinking I was sending the wrong signals to him, I started to lead him down to the ménage and tried lunging him, but these sessions ended up with him bucking round and round the school and then taking off flat out in a blind panic with me in the middle not being able to stop him. When we studied him, he was going down the lane hesitating all the time, looking for something to jump out on him and his eyes were not at all relaxed – he just seemed terrified. At this point we looked for someone that may be able to help us.'

Solution

After a period of stress, such as box rest or change of home, a horse's behaviour can change. One of the potential changes that can occur is that the horse appears to develop anxiety. This anxiety can be limited to certain objects or situations or can be generalised to his entire environment. In Dylan's case, he had developed a generalised anxiety and thus his flight response was active at times where there was no threat and in situations where it previously hadn't been. This caused Dylan's behaviour to become unpredictable on the ground and when ridden. As Dylan is over 17 hands high, this made his behaviour very dangerous for his owners. If your horse seems to be very spooky in situations which don't appear to be threatening, a similar dysfunction of the flight response may be occurring. In order to combat Dylan's unpredictable fear response and help him to calm down and regain self-control, it was necessary to counter condition his fear response with a calm and still response. The goal was for Dylan to learn to control his fear reaction in order to earn rewards. The rewards also help to give the horse something other than his anxiety to focus on and thus prevent his fear from spiralling out of control. After the calm response has been rewarded reliably over time, the horse will find it rewarding to control his own flight response, even when the handler is caught without a reward.

The first step to changing Dylan's flight response was to introduce him to clicker training. Clicker training is the easiest way to reward the horse quickly when he is producing the correct behaviour, especially if you can't give the horse the reward immediately, for example when riding or long lining. The click lets the horse know he is doing the correct behaviour and will be rewarded. This ensures that it is the behaviour clicked that is reinforced and not a behaviour that may occur a few seconds later when the treat arrives. This element of clicker training is particularly important when working with anxious horses, since only calm, controlled behaviour must be rewarded and reinforced.

Once Dylan understood the association between the click noise and the arrival of a reward, we applied the training to overcome his anxiety and overactive flight reflex. To start the process, we used an umbrella, an object Dylan is slightly nervous about. You should always start with an object that the horse is only slightly nervous about, so that you can concentrate on the timing of the click and reward with good calm behaviour without worrying about overly panicking the horse. At first the umbrella was only held and Dylan was rewarded for any calm and controlled behaviour displayed around the umbrella. If Dylan tried to run or leave the area he was controlled as gently as possible with the halter and then highly praised when he was once again controlled and calm. Don't get angry or rough with the horse if he tries to leave, as you will only escalate his fear. Once Dylan was happy with the umbrella, it was opened and shut in an increasingly unpredictable manner (this is built up so that some systematic desensitisation occurs and the horse is unlikely to panic). Again any attempt made by Dylan to remain controlled and calm was rewarded using the clicker training. Soon Dylan was controlling his flight response and staying calmly, regardless of how or where the umbrella was opened or moved to.

After this task it was important that the training was applied any time Dylan became afraid. The purpose of the training is not to desensitise the horse to everything in his environment, but to teach him to control his flight response should he feel anxiety about a situation or object. This is especially important with horses such as Dylan who have become generally fearful, rather than fearful of specific objects or situations. Desensitising Dylan to his whole environment would have been a very long process. Dylan's owners applied the training very well. Whenever he became scared but chose to stay calm and mindful of the handler, the click and treat was used to reward his efforts. The end result of this training is that Dylan's first response to a fearful situation will be to stay controlled and mindful of his handler, since this behaviour has been rewarded and become the dominant behavioural pattern in such circumstances. Be aware that this process will take a little time and there may be very occasional times where the behaviour reoccurs. If the fearful behaviour reoccurs, simply re-establish the training; as soon as the horse chooses to control himself, reward this behaviour (Fig. 12.6).

Figure 12.6   Dylan now a much calmer horse.

Finally if the horse goes through another period of stress (i.e. through box rest or a change of home) it may be necessary to re-establish his calm, controlled response as his first response to fearful events and objects in his environment.

MY TRAINING LOG — OVERCOMING FEARS

This training log can be used to record your progress and success when helping your horse to overcome any fears he may have.

Fear to Overcome	Date Started	Notes	Date Finished

Knowing Your Horse: A Guide to Equine Learning, Training and Behaviour
Emma Lethbridge
9781405191647

Learning with Character 13

One white foot, buy him
Two white feet, try him
Three white feet, look well about him
Four white feet, go home without him

We are all aware of the old wives' tales which marry horses' physical attributes and their psychological state. Some well-known examples are that chestnut mares are cantankerous, horses with one hair swirl on their heads are dependable but those with more than one are unpredictable, small eyes are a sign of stubbornness, or that horses with wall eyes or with the whites of the eyes showing are crazy. Every horse is different in both his physical and psychological characteristics, but can characteristics such as age, sex and breeding affect the horse's learning ability?

DOES THE SEX OF THE HORSE AFFECT LEARNING ABILITY?

In some species differences in spatial learning ability due to the sex of the animal have been found, with males being more proficient. Do any differences in learning occur in horses due to the sex of the animal? Murphy *et al.* (2004) investigated visual-spatial learning in horses; 34 males and 28 females took part in the study. The horses were tested on their ability to access a food source. In the test there were four stables located next to each other; in each stable was a feed bin and a moveable barrier. The breastplate height barriers were used to control access to the feed bins in three of the stables. There were six tests in all during the experiment. The authors found that male horses were able to complete trials significantly faster and locate the food source faster than females. Males could complete the six tests in a mean time of 30 s or less per test. They also committed a lower number of errors during the tests and were able to correctly navigate significantly more tests than female horses. This study would suggest that visual-spatial learning would be more efficient in males, as is found in other species including humans.

However, other studies have found no difference in the ability of male and female to learn spatial tasks. The learning of instrumental and spatial tasks by horses of between one and three years of age and of both sexes has been studied by Wolff and Hausberger (1996). In the instrumental learning task (the ability to open a chest), no difference was found between males or females. There was also no difference between the horses, regardless of age or sex, in their ability to memorise the task for the second test session, although interestingly, younger females did appear to learn faster overall. Wolff and Hausberger also found that in the spatial task more females than males were able to correctly complete the task. This is contrary to previous studies and the general trend found in other species.

So what do these studies mean in terms of practical training? Well, they seem to confirm that in the vast majority of tasks male and female horses can be trained in exactly the same manner and are equally able to perform learning tasks, memory tasks and possibly even equally able to complete spatial tasks. There is no bases to discriminate between male and female horses for training with regard to intellectual performance.

THE EFFECT OF AGE ON LEARNING ABILITY

We have all heard the phrase 'you can't teach an old dog new tricks' and although an exaggeration, this statement does have some truth to it. There is a trend in the majority of species for learning ability to decrease with advancing age. Correspondingly, Mader and Price (1980) found that there was a significant decrease in the horse's ability to learn a rewarded three-choice discrimination task the older the horse was. This was also found by Houpt et al. (1982) who found that the older the mare being studied, the slower she was able to successfully complete a maze learning task, i.e. to turn left in the maze, and furthermore, the slower she was at reversing the learning to learn to turn right in the maze. These studies seem to strongly indicate that the decrease in learning ability with age seen in other species is also true for horses and should be considered during training. When training the older horse it will be necessary to take longer and be more patient.

Age seems to also affect the attention span of the horse. A study by Rapin *et al.* (2007) investigated the horse's attention span using operant conditioning tasks. Once the horses had learned the task and signal, they were then asked to increase the time they were on task for and their attention span during the task was measured. The horses were then retested three weeks later. The study showed that the horses' age had a significant effect on their ability to hold their attention on the task. The young horses in the study were able to complete the first test with very good attention, but their attention would drop off on repetition of the task. The older horses were much more consistent in their ability to hold attention on a task and were even able to increase their attention span on repetition of the task. The sex and breed of the horse had no effect on attention time on this study. For practical application during training, these results imply that training sessions involving younger horses should be kept short and productive without unnecessary replication of tasks because of the likelihood that the young horse's attention span and performance will decrease as the task is repeated during training. It will also mean that they learn most efficiently at the beginning of task sessions.

DOES SOCIAL STATUS AFFECT LEARNING?

Social status plays a big role in natural and domesticated herds and in the life of the horse as a social being. Social status affects the ability of each horse to acquire and hold resources such as food, but are the horses at the top intellectually superior to their herd peers or just big dumb bullies?

The social status of the horse within the herd has been studied with regard to learning abilities. Haag *et al.* (1980) studied the effect of social status on the ability of horses to learn avoidance and maze learning tasks. Ten ponies were used in the study. The level of dominance and position in the herd hierarchy of each pony in the group was found by observing pairs of ponies competing for a feed bucket. The pony who could acquire and keep possession of the feed bucket was deemed to be the more dominant of the two ponies. The ponies were then tested on their ability to learn to avoid an electric shock and to learn a maze route to food. Social hierarchy had no effect on the ponies' ability to learn either of the tasks. Mader and Price (1980) also found that a horse's place in a social hierarchy had no effect on his ability to learn discrimination tasks. So it appears that learning ability is not required for, nor is a product of, social dominance within a herd.

NATURE VERSUS NURTURE

In all animals, including humans, it is often debated how much is innate (acquired from the DNA inherited from the parents) and how much is acquired from the environment. This is widely known as the nature versus nurture debate. This question of nature versus nurture could be asked of the learning ability of horses. How much of a horse's learning ability is acquired from their inherited DNA and how much is drawn from the horse's environment?

There is some evidence that learning ability may be at least in part inherited from the parents. For example, Wolff and Hausberger (1996) found that young horses from a particular stallion were significantly slower at learning to open a chest than the other young horses who took part in the study. In a spatial learning task taught as part of the same study, it was found that offspring of one particular stallion were much more successful at completing the learning task than the other young stock in the study. The observation that young stock from certain stallions have a greater or lesser ability to complete certain learning tasks suggests that a horse's genetic make-up acquired from one or other parent may have an influence on his ability with regard to different forms of learning. Not all studies confirm genetic influence on learning ability in horses. For example, Houpt *et al.* (1982) found that there was no correlation between the ability of a mare and her foal to learn a simple maze task. This lack of a link between the learning ability of the mare and her foal suggests that genetics may not be a factor in the horse's learning ability.

These confused results probably suggest a requirement for more research to be done into the possible inheritance of learning abilities in horses. As good learning ability is a desirable factor in any animal to be trained, it would be useful to find out whether it can be bred into the equine population and selected for, especially as most equine breeding is currently based around physical factors such as movement.

Given that the results for inheritance of learning abilities are unclear, is there any evidence that a horse's environment and early experiences can influence his learning ability? Interestingly, Houpt *et al*. (1982) found that orphaned foals, who had been deprived of normal maternal interaction and upbringing, did not have significantly affected ability to learn a maze task, although it was observed that they were slower at learning at the beginning of the task. Maternal bonding and interaction is a large part of a foal's early experience but there are other factors which could potentially affect the development of learning abilities. Heird *et al*. (1981) investigated the effect of human handling on the learning ability of young foals. Twenty four quarter horses were split into three groups; one group had very limited handling and human interaction, one group had an intermediate amount of handling and one group had an extensive amount of handling. When the foals reached approximately 14 months of age, they were conditioned to perform a T-shaped maze test which was rewarded with feed. Each horse underwent 30 trials that were done daily over a period of 20 days, with the location of the feed altered each day. The authors found that the intermediately handled foals learned fastest but all the handled horses did better than the unhandled. This information suggests that foal handling can potentially increase the horse's learning ability and is yet another argument for good early foal socialisation and training.

LEARNING RECAP

Overall, it can be concluded that horses should be treated as individuals during training. Stereotypes should be ignored as there is no evidence that learning ability is governed by sex or physical characteristics, although session lengths should be shortened when training young horses to accommodate their limited attention span. The methods described in this book can be applied with thought to the individual horse's learning preferences with great success, regardless of physical characteristics.

References and Further Reading

REFERENCES

Christensen, J.W., Rundgren, M. and Olsson, K. (2006) Training methods for horses: habituation to a frightening stimulus. *Equine Veterinary Journal*, **38**(5), 439–443.

Christensen, J.W., Zharkikh, T. and Ladewig, J. (2008a) Do horses generalise between objects during habituation? *Applied Animal Behaviour Science*, **114**(3–4), 509–520.

Christensen, J.W., Malmkvist, J., Nielsen, B.L. and Keeling, L.J. (2008b) Effects of a calm companion on fear reactions in naïve test horses. *Equine Veterinary Journal*, **40**(1), 46–50.

Haag, E.L., Rudman, R. and Houpt, K.A. (1980) Avoidance, maze learning and social dominance in ponies. *Journal of Animal Science*, **50**, 329–335.

Hanggi, E. (2003) Discrimination learning based on relative size concepts in horses (*Equus caballus*). *Applied Animal Behaviour Science*, **83**(3), 201.

Heird, J.C., Lennon, A.M. and Bell, R.W. (1981) Effects of early experience on the learning ability of yearling horses. *Journal of Animal Science*, **53**, 1204–1209.

Heleski, C., Bauson, L. and Bello, N. (2008) Evaluating the addition of positive reinforcement for learning a frightening task: a pilot study with horses. *Journal of Applied Animal Welfare Science*, **11**(3), 213–222.

Houpt, K.A., Parsons, M.S. and Hintz, H.F. (1982) Learning ability of orphan foals, of normal foals and of their mothers. *Journal of Animal Science*, **55**, 1027–1032.

Innes, L. and McBride, S. (2007) Negative versus positive reinforcement: an evaluation of training strategies for rehabilitated horses. *Applied Animal Behaviour Science*, **112**, 357–368.

Lansade, L., Bertrand, M., Boivin, X. and Bouissou, M.F. (2003) Effects of handling at weaning on manageability and reactivity of foals. *Applied Animal Behaviour Science*, **87**, 131–149.

Lansade, L., Bertrand, M. and Bouissou, M.F. (2004) Effects of neonatal handling on subsequent manageability, reactivity and learning ability of foals. *Applied Animal Behaviour Science*, **93**, 143–158.

Mader, D.R. and Price, E.O. (1980) Discrimination learning in horses: effects of breed, age and social dominance. *Journal of Animal Science*, **50**, 962–965.

Mairinger, F. (1997) *Horses Are Made to be Horses*. Howell Books, John Wiley, Chichester.

Martin, J.A. (1977) Effects of positive and negative adult–child interactions on children's task performance and task preferences. *Journal of Experimental Child Psychology*, **23**, 493–502.

McCall, C.A. and Burgin, S.E. (2002) Equine utilization of secondary reinforcement during response extinction and acquisition. *Applied Animal Behaviour Science*, **78**(4), 253.

Murphy, J., Waldmann, T. and Arkins, S. (2004) Sex differences in equine learning skills and visuo-spatial ability. *Applied Animal Behaviour Science*, **87**, 119–130.

Ninomiya, S., Mitsumasu, T., Aoyama, M. and Kusunose, R. (2007) A note on the effect of a palatable food reward on operant conditioning in horses. *Applied Animal Behaviour Science*, **108**, 342–347.

Rapin, V., Poncet, P.A., Burger, D., Mermod, C. and Richard, M.A. (2007) Measurement of the attention time in the horse. *Schweiz Arch Tierheilkd*, **149**(2), 77–83.

Rubin, L., Oppegard, C. and Hintz, H.F. (1980) The effect of varying the temporal distribution of conditioning trials on equine learning behaviour. *Journal of Animal Science*, **50**, 1184–1187.

Sappington, B.F. and Goldman, L. (1994) Discrimination learning and concept formation in the Arabian horse. *Journal of Animal Science*, **72**(12), 3080–3087.

Schultz, W. (1998) Predictive reward signal of dopamine neurons. *Journal of Neurophysiology*, **80**(1), 1–27.

Simpson, B.S. (2002) Neonatal foal handling. *Applied Animal Behaviour Science*, **78**, 303–317.

Smith, S. and Goldman, L. (1998) Colour discrimination in horses. *Applied Animal Behaviour Science*, **62**(1), 13–25.

Warren-Smith, A.K. and McGreevy, P.D. (2007) The use of blended positive and negative reinforcement in shaping the halt response of horses (*Equus caballus*). *Animal Welfare*, **16**(4), 481–488.

Warren-Smith, A.K and McGreevy, P.D. (2008) Equestrian coaches' understanding and application of learning theory in horse training. *Antrozoos*, **21**(2), 153–162.

Williams, J.L., Friend, T.H., Toscano, M.J., Collins, M.N., Sisto-Burt, A. and Nevill, C.H. (2002) The effects of early training sessions on the reactions of foals at 1, 2, and 3 months of age. *Applied Animal Behaviour Science*, **77**(2), 105.

Williams, J.L., Friend, T.H., Collins, M.N., Toscano, M.J., Sisto-Burt, A. and Nevill, C.H. (2003) Effects of imprint training procedure at birth on the reactions of foals at age six months. *Equine Veterinary Journal*, **35**(2), 127–132.

Williams, J.L., Friend, T., Nevill, C. and Archer, G. (2004) The efficacy of a secondary reinforcer (clicker) during acquisition and extinction of an operant task in horses. *Applied Animal Behaviour Science*, **88**, 331–341.

Wolff, A. and Hausberger, M. (1996) Learning and memorisation of two different tasks in horses: the effects of age, sex and sire. *Applied Animal Behaviour Science*, **46**(3), 137–143.

FURTHER READING

The following are books and papers I recommend as further reading to extend your knowledge from this book.

Budiansky, S. (1998) *The Nature of Horses: Their Evolution, Intelligence and Behaviour*. Phoenix, London. A great book exploring equine perception and intelligence, a useful read for any owner or trainer.

Kiley-Worthington, M. (1997) *The Behaviour of Horses in Relation to Management and Training*, Chapter 9. J.A. Allen, London. A nice summary chapter of the basic concepts of learning theory. As a whole the book is also a good introduction to equine behaviour.

Kurland, A. (2007) *Clicker Training for Your Horse*. Sunshine Books, Washington. A great book to help any trainer start to apply clicker training to their equine activities.

Lieberman, D.A. (2000) *Learning, Behavior and Cognition*. Wadsworth, Belmont, California. This is a great academic book covering all aspects of learning and behaviour and is a good read or reference book for students or any scientifically minded horse trainer.

Mills, D. and McDonnell, S. (2005) *The Domestic Horse: The Evolution, Development and Management of its Behaviour*. Cambridge University Press, Cambridge. This is a very in-depth book about the nature of horses, their behaviour and how they should be managed to best meet their innate needs in domestication.

Mills, D. and Nankervis, K. (1999) *Equine Behaviour: Principles and Practice*, Chapter 9. Blackwell Publishing, Oxford. Again, a nice summary of the principles surrounding training horses using learning theory. The book as a whole is also a good insight into equine behaviour.

Pryor, K. (1994) *Lads Before the Wind: Diary of a Dolphin Trainer*. Sunshine Books, Washington. This is an easy and captivating read about the author's adventures setting up a sea life centre and being one of the first applying operant and classical conditioning to train sea mammals for shows and management purposes. *Don't Shoot the Dog* by Karen Pryor is also a valuable read.

Index